BERKLEE PRESS

T0081346

MUSIC
smarts

The INSIDE TRUTH and
ROAD-TESTED WISDOM
from the BRIGHTEST MINDS
in the MUSIC BUSINESS

MR. BONZAI
Edited by David Schwartz

With a Grace
Note by
GRAHAM
NASH

Berklee Press

Vice President: David Kusek
Dean of Continuing Education: Debbie Cavalier
Chief Operating Officer: Robert F. Green
Managing Editor: Jonathan Feist
Editorial Assistants: Emily Goldstein, Rajasri Mallikarjuna, Adrienne Dinnall
Cover Designer: Kathy Kikkert
Photographs by Mr. Bonzai, except where otherwise noted

ISBN 978-0-87639-097-9

1140 Boylston Street
Boston, MA 02215-3693 USA
(617) 747-2146

Visit Berklee Press Online at
www.berkleepress.com

DISTRIBUTED BY

HAL•LEONARD®
CORPORATION
7777 W. BLUEMOUND RD. P.O. BOX 13819
MILWAUKEE, WISCONSIN 53213
Visit Hal Leonard Online at
www.halleonard.com

For Keiko,
the sculptor of my dreams

CONTENTS

A GRACE NOTE BY GRAHAM NASH

This world is powered by images and energy. What Mr. Bonzai did here was to present a small slice of our musical heritage—a slice that includes many of my personal heroes. Look into these faces, seek out their stories, and enjoy this wonderful, insightful journey.

Graham Nash
Los Angeles, CA
August 24th, 2008

PREFACE

My musical odyssey began on September 29, 1967, when I walked into Abbey Road recording studios as a guest of John Lennon, who introduced me to George, Paul, Ringo, George Martin, Neil Aspinall, Peter Brown, and Mal Evans. It was the night the finishing touches were being recorded for "I Am the Walrus." As the lone outsider, I heard snippets of other songs, too, all of which I knew were predestined to become part of our eventual consciousness. I witnessed a musical powerhouse, yet one that was as low-key as your grandma's kitchen.

You might say I spied a signpost. The road led to over 500 formal interviews, clandestine meetings, outrageous lunchings, startling conversations on the hoof, and happenstance encounters to collect what lies before you. Herein are spur of the moment ejaculations, witty nuggets, and solemn judgments, cherry-picked from over a million words, not to mention some provocative photo sessions.

Step into this gallery of the musical life, lined with intriguing reflections on heroes, influences, artistic integrity, improvisation, collaboration, performance, recording, power, money, fame, and rejection—all in one bountiful bento box stocked with hard-won wisdom, surprising pratfalls, stark realizations, and not what you might expect.

I hope you enjoy and are enriched by these crystal quotations. I am continuously inspired when fellow humans show me their faces and tell me their stories.

With gassho, and all my bows and ribbons.

Mr. Bonzai
Hollywood, California
August 29, 2008

1

MUSIC MAKES THE WORLD GO 'ROUND

FOR THE LOVE OF IT

THE RIGHT PLACE

I really discourage a lot of people from getting into this racket. I don't think it's something you should get into for the money. You should get into it because you just love to do it.

—*Dr. John*

JUST PLAY

Just play every chance you get, for anyone who will listen.

—*Willie Nelson*

THE GIRL CAN'T HELP IT

I don't think true musicians, actors, and artists have any choice.

—*k.d. lang*

WAY BACK IN THE DAY

Nothing has really changed in the creation of music since that first guy started beating on a log and that woman found a reed with holes and blew in it and got a whistling sound. You immerse yourself in the energy of the universe and pluck your note.

—*Ray Manzarek*

k.d. lang

LOVE IS WHAT WE NEED

Pet Sounds was the love album. It had love in it, and I think people need that. A lot of people don't want to admit it, but they need that kind of a spiritual love that we put out there in our records.
—*Brian Wilson*

WITHIN AND WITHOUT

What we have always tried to do as artists is to reflect what is going on around us and reveal what is going on inside of us.
—*Graham Nash*

A HIGHER LOVE

When you play a song, whether for a couple people sitting around in a room or thousands of people at a concert, you get on the same wavelength where it feels like you agree with someone—where you have a common ground. Music can unite people.
—*Jack Johnson*

Jack Johnson

SPINAL TIP

Be patient. Remember, they're not going to like you automatically just because *you* do.
—*David St. Hubbins*

THE HEART OF THE MATTER

You have to love music for itself. If you get into it because it's cool, or you want to be like whoever the current person is that year, then it won't last, and you're taking up everybody else's time.

—*Suzanne Vega*

Suzanne Vega

KEEP IT UP

Being a musician is a lifelong thing. If you have the right temperament and the right amount of drive, there's no reason you can't continually work.

—*Max Weinberg*

IT'S ONLY NATURAL

Music has always existed in nature—the percussion of rain, the rustling of branches in the wind, the voices of animals. When people get together, it's our nature to make music.

—*Terry Becker*

LOVE YOUR MUSIC

We never get tired of the music we made in the sixties, which is just the opposite of guys who say, "If I have to play that song one more time, I'm gonna shoot myself." We're lucky. It could have been music that we *weren't* crazy about.

—*Steve Cropper*

THANK YOUR LUCKY STARS

I wake up every day feeling so lucky that I can have this much fun doing what I do, working with people and their music. I thank my lucky stars every day.

—*Mike Shipley*

TIMELESSNESS

Les Paul's ideas and the music he makes will always be there. It was quite a moment when I looked him in the eye and saw how he loved doing what he does.
—*David Lindley*

BEING PAUL McCARTNEY

Paul is a musician's musician. He'd rather hang out with a musician than the Queen of England. He just truly loves making music.
—*David Foster*

David Lindley

THE GOOD FIGHT

I'm just a crusader of music for music's sake.
—*Al Kooper*

FROM THE HEART

Play music from the bottom of your heart, as good as you can do it.
—*Patti Cathcart*

PLAY FOR KEEPS

I know that if I fall flat on my face commercially, I can always play. And no time I've spent playing will ever be wasted. It's good for you. It's like food.
—*Leo Kottke*

Patti Cathcart

HEROES

FANTASY BEATLE

When I saw the Beatles on the Ed Sullivan show, music became something really great. For a long time, I fantasized that I was the fifth Beatle. When each one needed to take a break while on stage, they would just nod at me, and I would jump up and fill in without missing a beat.

—*Mark Mothersbaugh*

Mark Mothersbaugh

MILES OF STYLES

Miles has been my main influence all the way back to when I first heard him as a child. I would listen to his records and then go see him live, and the music would be radically different—faster, more complex, and had stuff I'd never heard on records. I realized you don't always have to go out and play the record.

—*George Duke*

A MOVING EXPERIENCE

Seeing Jimi Hendrix perform was a very powerful experience for me. He had a way of moving when he played: he moved in space unlike anybody I had ever seen. He seemed to sit in the atoms differently than we did.

—*Rickie Lee Jones*

MAKING ROOM FOR OTHERS

When I started playing with other musicians, I started listening to Nat Cole and Errol Garner, two masters of the swing piano. Nat was a model for pianists who play well with a bass and drums. He left room for the other musicians.

—*Mose Allison*

Mose Allison

MEETING HEROES

Bob Dylan spoke of the end of idolatry after he met Woody Guthrie. By meeting them, it makes those artists not only human, but often less than human. You see that all the pieces don't have to be there. That's what can make them unique—their limitations.

—*David Was*

COOLNESS

Jimi Hendrix gave me all the lessons in coolness I will need for the rest of my life.

—*Anthony Kiedis*

FRANKIE

For lyric interpretation, pronunciation, intonation—and the actual sound of his voice, Sinatra is the best there is.

—*Harry Connick, Jr.*

CLAPTON

In my opinion, Eric Clapton is the greatest rock 'n' roll guitarist alive. Nobody has given him anything. He earned it.

—*B.B. King*

A CLASSIC RECORDING

I really respect Bruce Swedien. In 1959, he made one of the defini-tive classical recordings—the 2001

B.B. King

theme, "Also Sprach Zarathustra" with Fritz Reiner and the Chicago Symphony. A remarkable classical recording that still stands out today as incredible.

—*Allen Sides*

HAL'S TALKING DRUMS

Hal Blaine had everything: sound, feel, and style, and had it perfectly proportioned. He didn't play very hard. You can hear it, like on the Mamas and Papas records, a lot of very subtle stuff. He had great ideas and execution and the confidence to say to everyone around him, "This is right," whether he was saying it verbally, or through his drums.

—*Max Weinberg*

THE KING OF SLIDE

Nobody is funkier than David Lindley. And there is so much pathos when he is playing quiet stuff. He's one of the most dangerous slide players that ever lived.

—*Jackson Browne*

Jackson Browne

JIMI'S ART

Hendrix painted pictures with sound, and he wasn't copying anybody. There was a magic about him—an aura that hasn't been matched.
—*Steve Lukather*

YOUNG ARETHA

I remember Aretha when she was ten or eleven years old, singing on the radio from her father's church. She's always been number one for me, for her creative and vocal genius. She's the greatest singer I've ever heard.
—*Brian Holland*

THE INIMITABLE MR. ARMSTRONG

Harry Connick, Jr,

Anybody can be imitated to some extent, except for Louis Armstrong, and maybe Charlie Parker and Art Tatum. Louis never went that far away from the melody, but he dealt with such musical complexities—harmonically, rhythmically, thematically— that he took the simplest of songs and made them into unbelievable masterpieces.
—*Harry Connick, Jr.*

ELVIS COULD DANCE

The first time I saw *Jailhouse Rock*, I was stunned. That choreographed dance scene in the prison cell blocks was amazing, unbelievable—one of the most charismatic moments in rock 'n' roll history.
—*Dwight Yoakam*

AGAINST THE ODDS

I loved Patsy Cline's voice, the emotion, humor, and power. She was a very progressive woman trying to make it in this business. I guess I related to her in a sense—a woman struggling against the odds.
—*k.d. lang*

SPEAKING FRANKLY

Frank Zappa was completely non-compromising with his artistic vision, which is the only way a truly historical musician can be. And he was bulletproof when it came to being honest. He never said he was going to do something and then didn't do it. People that knew Frank loved him.
—*Steve Vai*

Steve Vai

INFLUENCES

CHUCK IN MY SOUL

Chuck Berry was one of our greatest songwriters. "Johnny B. Goode" was the first song of his I heard. I was in my car, and when that came on, I flipped out. I pulled over and stopped. The electricity of it just got me in my soul, in my blood.
—*Brian Wilson*

Brian Wilson

LES CHANGED THINGS

One record, in my estimation, forever changed popular music—Les Paul and Mary Ford's *How High the Moon*. It broke through like a shining light. All of a sudden, it was no longer necessary to present popular music in concert-like form. It was perfectly all right to bend reality. On that record, there is only one instrument and one voice. Les Paul plays all the instrumental parts, and Mary Ford sings all the vocal parts. There isn't a shred of reality on that record. With its tremendous popularity, pop music took a big turn.
—*Bruce Swedien*

THE BEBOP MESSAGE

Shortly after the war, the guys from my generation, in '45 and '46 in Belgium, started to get these records—78s with this explosive bebop message from Dizzy Gillespie and Charlie Parker. That influenced me totally. I couldn't imagine anything more important happening in my life.

—*Toots Thielemans*

Toots Thielemans

GETTING IT

Joe Cocker turned me on to rock 'n' roll. I didn't really understand it—didn't see what all the to-do was about until he joined the label around 1969, the time of the *Mad Dogs and Englishmen* tour. They were rehearsing on our sound stage, and one afternoon I decided to watch them working. He was totally into it, and the drummer was churning out this unbelievable motor, and . . . I got the message.

—*Herb Alpert*

BLUES POWER

The piano work on the Chuck Berry records is textbook blues playing. He and Otis Spann were my two biggest influences.

—*Al Kooper*

REAL MUSIC

Fifties radio in Macon, Georgia had the most amazing music I had ever heard. I was coming out of a classical background, but then I heard early r&b from guys who went down to juke joints in the backwoods and recorded musicians who could *really* play. It was a startling experience for me—real music with honesty.
—*George Massenburg*

George Massenburg

JAZZ WITH A COWBOY HAT

When I heard Bob Wills, I realized I could wear a cowboy hat and play jazz! The feeling of playing this music is like getting high.
—*Ray Benson*

REVELATIONS

The people that really blew my mind—that changed me radically and constantly—were Bob Dylan, the Beatles, the Stones, Van Morrison, and Joni Mitchell—writers who plumbed the depth of their experience and revealed things about all of our lives.
—*Jackson Browne*

AT THE FEET OF A MASTER

Bruce Swedien helped me get my first job as an apprentice in Chicago, and I worked for him as an assistant. If I'm any good now, it has a great deal to do with the time I got to sit behind him.
—*Ed Cherney*

Ed Cherney

DEAL WITH THE REAL WORLD

The musicians who have inspired me—people like Herbie Hancock, Wayne Shorter, Miles Davis, Ornette Colman, Wes Montgomery, Paul Bley—what they all have in common is that they deal with whatever is happening in their world in a very immediate, spontaneous, and creative way.

—*Pat Metheny*

TRADITIONAL SONGS

There is such strength in traditional music. Compare a typical pop song with a Scottish ballad—no question which is the greater song. It's been sung for hundreds of years, and all the bad verses have been dropped. The language is refined—so strong, colorful, and immediate. So much is conveyed in one verse.

—*Richard Thompson*

IT JUST GOES TO SHOW YOU

My favorite live album is *Ray Charles in Person*, and legend has it that it was taken off a single microphone from someone in the audience with a good machine.

—*Russ Titelman*

CREEDENCE CLEARWATER REVIVED COUNTRY

It was something I could listen to without being ostracized by the kids in Columbus, Ohio. It was country, but it was cool. Fogerty came from a pure place and recaptured the hip mystique in the bare bones of original country music.

—*Dwight Yoakam*

IT'S OK

Duke Ellington showed me that it was okay to be fanatical about my work.
—*Bruce Swedien*

PRINCE OF PERSISTENCE

Prince is the most talented person I've ever worked with. As a writer, performer, and artist, he is able to manifest these visions. Seeing his determination and clarity for what he wants was one of the big influences in my life.
—*David Tickle*

Bruce Swedien

BIRD'S LANGUAGE

Bird gave us the whole way of how to phrase and change the 2/4 pulse to the 4/4 pulse. Plus, he was an improvisational genius. Raw, pure energy poured out of him. Bird's language—the way that the music is spoken—changed the whole goddam planet.
—*Phil Woods*

LISTEN CLOSELY

Phil Ramone taught me that when you hear something you don't like, you go out and listen in the room, and move the microphone instead of moving the equalizer. Hearing his incredible work, with very little EQ and limiting, just blew me away.
—*Shelly Yakus*

GET A LITTLE CRAZY

My heroes—rebels like John Cage and Karlheinz Stockhausen—inspire me to do crazy things.
—*Brian "BT" Transeau*

REMEMBERING RAY

I've admired Ray Charles so much for so long. The way he played piano and organ meant so much to me. It was the deciding factor in determining what I was going to do with my life.
—*Booker T. Jones*

Booker T. Jones

LISTEN UP

"A Hundred Pounds of Clay," by Gene McDaniels—that was one of the first songs that made me sit up straight and start to listen carefully.
—*Paul Shaffer*

MUSICAL COMEDY

Through the Dr. Demento radio show, I got introduced to great things by Spike Jones, Stan Freberg, Tom Lehrer, Allen Sherman, and Ray Stevens. There wasn't anything else like it on the radio at the time.
—*"Weird Al" Yankovic*

SCI-FI ROOTS

I remember becoming aware of music in the prime of my sci-fi horror days— ages ten to thirteen. I realized at one point that all of my favorite sci-fi movies had the same film composer, Bernard Herrmann. He was a very big influence for me.
—*Danny Elfman*

Danny Elfman

BEING INSTRUMENTAL

TRUMPET PLAYERS

I don't know if trumpet players need to be the center of attention, but I think we need to be heard. The trumpet is not one of those instruments that you can hide behind. Before the electric guitar was cranked up, the trumpet player was the guitar player of yesteryear. He got all the women, too.

—*Herb Alpert*

THE DRUMMERS' ADVANTAGE

Achieving proficiency with the drums is relatively easy when compared to violin, for instance. With violin, you get no reward until you've been playing for two or three years. It takes that long to make a nice sound, let alone play music. With drums, the gratification is instant.

—*Stewart Copeland*

Stewart Copeland

AIR FIDDLE

In the 1920s and before, the population was about seventy percent rural. The fiddle was the lead instrument, and if you were a cool guy and wanted to get the girls, that's what you played.

—*Ray Benson*

THAT GUITAR SOUND

I experimented with the Gretsch Chet Atkins guitar I bought when I was seventeen, and learned that the bass strings were more powerful for recording than the treble strings. For that real dark powerful sound, I played the melody on the low strings, which became my ominous signature sound.

—*Duane Eddy*

Duane Eddy

ECONOMY PICKING

I do what I call "economy picking," where when you enter from one string to the next string, you always enter on a downstroke. That way, you can play runs twice as fast.

—*Tommy Tedesco*

BREAK 'EM IN

Generally, I like guitars more after I've had them for a while. I encourage people to drop them and kick them around. New guitars have that uncomfortable five-year break-in period.

—*Pat Metheny*

THE ORIGINAL CONDUCTOR

In Beethoven's time, the conductor was just a guy who stood in front of the orchestra with a stick and beat tempo. Wagner and Mendelssohn started the art of conducting facing the orchestra. Up to that time, everything was in the hands of the concertmaster and the first instrument of each group.

—*Carmine Coppola*

SLOW IS HARD

Some of the hardest classical pieces to play are slow movements in a sonata or symphony. Everything is exposed—your phrasing, your breath control, your intonation—and you can't hide behind anything.
—*Paul Horn*

Paul Horn

PLAYING UNDER PRESSURE

French horn is a difficult instrument to play. Most of the time in symphonic works, the player sits there counting bars for five minutes and then comes up to some difficult answers, or some solo—important interventions. These guys go crazy. There are some strange people among French horn players.
—*Toots Thielemans*

FIRST SYNTH

The electric guitar is the first heavily processed musical instrument— the first synthesizer. It can provide so many elements and still have that human sensitivity.
—*Danny Kortchmar*

THE NATURE OF MUSICAL INSTRUMENTS

Instruments have in their invention the nature of a character. They sound masculine or feminine, or neuter— and usually they have a national character. I use them very circumspectly, trying to observe their values.
—*Van Dyke Parks*

Van Dyke Parks

HOW'S THE BASS?

I've always loved the fact that a good bass line with the melody line can work incredibly well for an audience. They may not know why, but it really makes the difference, and it carries the groove.

—*Phil Ramone*

THE HENDRIX EXPERIENCE

Jimi was about staying open-minded and letting the sounds take you on a journey.

—*Eddie Kramer*

LESS IS MORE

It isn't always how much you play, but how much you don't play. Rick Danko used to say, "I don't play bass; I play space."

—*Eddy Offord*

Eddie Kramer

BASS SIGNATURE

Where a lot of guys are very articulate in the way they address notes, I tend to do glissandos more. I slide between notes, and play with a greasier style. Because of old hand injuries, my middle two fingers really don't work that well, so most of my playing is my first and fourth fingers, and sliding makes it easier to get to a note. If I have any signature, maybe that's it.

—*Leland Sklar*

FIND YOUR GROOVE

The best thing that a drummer can do is find the groove—the groove that works for that song. This is what the masters of drumming do.

—*Max Weinberg*

PLAY TO THE SONG

I listen to the lyrics and fit the dynamics of my playing to the meaning of the song. This used to cause problems with engineers, who wanted me to play at consistent levels so they could adjust the volume in the control room.

—*Hal Blaine*

Hal Blaine

THE BIGGEST PART

Listening is the biggest part of playing music.

—*Jim Keltner*

CHANNELING MUSIC

When I play I get absorbed in the music so that I'm lost, almost in a trance, but still aware. I want the music to come through me in a very open, clear way, as if I am a channel.

—*Paul Horn*

PLAY IN THE MOMENT

What I've seen as a producer is a small handful of guys like Keith Richards, Willie Nelson, and Bob Dylan, who know how to let go and play in the moment, and not think about it. They lose musical self-consciousness.

—*Don Was*

SERIOUS OR MAD?

I find a great kind of madness common among some musicians. You can tell they have an appetite for what they love to do. They chew on it; they eat it up.

—*David Lindley*

UNDERSTAND YOUR ARTIST

In James Taylor's case, the part he writes for the guitar to accompany himself is very often the basis of the arrangement of the song. One of the mistakes you can make is putting too much on top of that and losing the guitar and the chord changes that he puts underneath the melody.

—*Peter Asher*

Peter Asher

BE TRUE TO YOURSELF

Miles Davis once said, "I am the first one to know if I sound good or bad, and very often the only one." Just because you get a standing ovation doesn't mean that you played well. You are the one who knows if what you tried to play came out or not. That's jazz.

—*Toots Thielemans*

THE RIGHT TO RECORD

I've never performed professionally. I figure that people who are interested in the recording business have a right to make a living making records.

—*Harry Nilsson*

COMPATIBILITY

Music is a universal language. Two musicians from completely different walks of life can talk about how much punch is on a snare drum, and know what they are talking about.

—*Thomas Dolby*

MUSICIAN'S POV

I'm still working to get it together as a musician. That's what inspires me—the idea of looking at the world that I live in as a musician and expressing a larger picture of what I'm interested in over the course of a whole series of records.

—*Pat Metheny*

THE BAND

BAND DYNAMICS

In a band situation, you become a creature of habit. You have certain ways of relating, power structures build up, and negotiating skills are required.

—*Peter Gabriel*

TOGETHERNESS

You can't replace that synergy that happens when musicians play together. When I'm playing with a jazz group, the tendency is to use the creative powers of the other members of the group. I write something minimal so we can get right into the improvising.

—*Herbie Hancock*

Herbie Hancock

GETTING TO KNOW YOU

As bands get to know each other, they have problems and hidden agendas that must be resolved—both musically and personality-wise. Somebody has to be there to keep it together.

—*Phil Ramone*

UNSPOKEN

Musicians that play together for a long time have a certain empathy and understanding—more than you can put down in notes. It's like when two people live together for a while, and get to know each other so well that there's a communication that's almost mystical.

—*Paul Horn*

DRUM ROLE

There's a love and a respect for each other that comes out in our music. I just want to lay a nice foundation for these guys to paint their musical expressions on. That's my role, and it makes me feel good.

—*Chad Smith*

Chad Smith

DIY

I've always wished that I was in a band, although everyone I ever said that to, who was in a band, said "No, you don't, man. You *don't* want to be in a band."

—*Jackson Browne*

HIGH STANDARDS

What we enjoy about each other is that we all have very high standards and are extremely critical. We all have areas in which we are good, and at this point, we have psyched out what they are. We shift very quickly and easily from one person to another being in charge.

—*Pat Metheny*

THE CSN&Y OPERATING PLAN

We started out by saying, "Listen, this is just four guys. We are not a 'band.' We will make music with whomever we wish, because we are following our hearts, and our musical instincts, chasing the muse down."

—*Graham Nash*

FRANK'S BAND

He hired people who were at the top of their skill level, and trained them to do extraordinary things under his baton. He would always allow them to have some space in the show to present what he called, "Body Commercials"—his terminology for solos. If someone was capable of something unique, he would always find a way to expose and exploit it.
—*Dweezil Zappa*

Dweezil Zappa

PLAYING ON E STREET

We're street musicians, schooled in the bars and joints of New Jersey where there isn't a lot of technical prowess. You could find better players—more technically proficient guys—but you would never find any musicians who play with more feeling, or who believe as strongly in the music they are playing. Nobody lays back in this band.
—*Max Weinberg*

SHARE THE SPOTLIGHT

Part of my job as a bandleader means being a politician. I have to make sure everyone gets their solo.
—*Mark Hudson*

Mark Hudson

GROUP VS. SOLO

Record making with a band is like movie making in some ways. Working on solo projects is more like painting, where you've got a canvas, and you start off with a certain intent. But because it's a quiet and intuitive process, the work starts to speak to you, often taking you off in a direction you didn't expect.

—*Lindsey Buckingham*

THE AUDIENCE

WE ALL LIKE MUSIC

People are the same all over the world. There may be religious, cultural, philosophical, and racial barriers, but they are transcended when you get up and play some music.

—*Paul Horn*

UNDER THE RADAR

I take great delight circulating in the audience before the show because nobody knows what I look like. I go back and check if the T-shirts are selling, have a drink, and watch people come in. They never know who I am. I kind of revel in that.

—*Alan Parsons*

Alan Parsons

RESPECT THE LISTENERS

Just about everybody loves music. Regardless of whether it's the singer or the listener, it's all music. I used to think that the people in the industry were the only ones with all the brains, and the listeners were the stupid people that couldn't make music, but could just hear it. It's not so.

—*Brian Wilson*

DO IT FOR THEM

We'll do the two-hour sound check even when we're dead tired so that it sounds good when people get in there. You think you can have a rock 'n' roll lifestyle, party all night, and then skip sound check? That kind of attitude shows up, and the audience catches it. Pretty soon, they fire you.

—*Chris Isaak*

BEAT 'EM TO THE PUNCH

I think performance is a way of expressing aggression. I find that you have to attack the audience, sometimes—do a pre-emptive strike and get to the audience's airfields before they can start throwing tomatoes at you.

—*Richard Thompson*

THE DOORS ON STAGE

When the music was right and Jim was right and everyone in the audience was of a like mind, it was fucking magic. Time would stop.

—*Ray Manzarek*

PLEASING THE CROWD OF OLD

In the nineteenth century and before, people often clapped after every movement, and if a particular

Ray Manzarek

movement—usually the scherzo—was a real crowd pleaser, they would applaud until the orchestra repeated it, before going on with the rest of the symphony.

—*Peter Schickele*

"ENTERTAINER" VERSUS "ARTIST"

The entertainer is out to please people. The more people he pleases, the happier he is. The artist does what he has to do. He hopes people will be pleased and pay him so he can make a living. If not, he still has to do it.

—*Artie Shaw*

BEING IN A CULT BAND

I think with any group that has enig-matic qualities within the aspects of "cult" status, there is a feeling in the audience—"Hey, I know something that the rest of the world isn't hip to." There's a certain pleasure to turning people on to that type of thing.

—*Bill Payne*

Bill Payne

GETTING STARTED

FIRST MUSIC

A GUY WITH A GUITAR

For me, it all started when I was six and my older brother brought home *Heartbreak Hotel*. It was a revelation. I was suddenly hit with that song, and the image of a guy with a guitar.
—*Lindsey Buckingham*

DISCOVERING MUSIC

The first time I was really aware of music was when I was ten years old and we visited some friends who had a player piano. They put rolls in it, and the keys went up and down. I watched, and finally I walked over and pushed some keys, and it happened. It impressed me so much. I started picking out little things.
—*Henry Mancini*

Henry Mancini

BEGINNINGS

I wrote down my first piece of music when I was seven, and it was called "March." There were two sections to the march: one was like a lion, and one was like a lamb.
—*Van Dyke Parks*

THE COMFORTS OF HOME

The first music I remember hearing was my grandfather, the choral director, rehearsing the town church choir in the living room every week. Grandma would make coffee and cookies. It was like going to church, except you could go to the bathroom whenever you wanted to.

—S. "Husky" Höskulds

GETTING AN EARLY START

I remember singing when I was only the height of the adults' kneecaps— singing to those kneecaps.

—Neil Finn

FIRST RECORDS

The first record I conned my mother into buying was *Rock Around the Clock*. She thought I'd learn how to tell time.

—Terry Becker

Neil Finn

MY FIRST GUITAR

The first one I ever tried was a friend's Elvis Presley plastic guitar with one string. I learned all the Shadows songs with one string, up and down the neck like a dervish.

—Jeff Lynne

STARTING WITH THE BEATLES

The first thing I actually remembered hearing was the *Meet the Beatles* record. My folks told me that I used to walk around with a pencil stuck in the center of the record, spinning it and trying to say the word "music!"
—*John Paterno*

John Paterno

THE LEARNING CURVE

FINDING YOUR WAY

I taught myself to read music, which is really pretty rational. If you know where one note is and one line, you can figure out the rest. I discovered where middle C was—under the S in "Steinway."

—*Suzanne Ciani*

Suzanne Ciani

KNOW THE NOTES

I don't see how some people try to become producers or engineers with no background in music. You're dealing with music constantly. You've got to know music. Otherwise, you'd just get lost.

—*Bob Clearmountain*

MULTITASK

Try to be as well-rounded as you can be. Don't think that one thing will make or break you. If you can do many things in these modern times, it's the best way you can survive.

—*Tom Biller*

EAR TRAINING

You have to train your ears by listening. And when you get tired in a session, you have to quit, because your ears can play tricks on you. The mind can retain a sound image for about ten seconds, and when you try to compare the next sound, you can lose the memory of the first sound. You have to train your ear to understand that.

—Bill Porter

THE LANGUAGE OF RECORDING

By listening to a lot of recordings, you begin to notice the ones that really seem to communicate the best and are most effective. It's a combination of the performance, the balances, the way it was mixed, the cleanness, and the way the soundstage is created.

—Bernie Grundman

ORIGINALITY

Maybe I'm fortunate to have a limited education. It's forced me to come up with my own ways.

—Jack Nitzsche

EVERYONE'S A TEACHER

I was like a sponge and hung out with anyone who could play. I'd learn what I could from them and then find someone else who was better.

—Steve Lukather

Jack Nitzsche

LEARNING FROM FAILURE

Nobody ever learns from success; you learn from failure. If you don't make mistakes, you'll never learn anything.
—*Artie Shaw*

Artie Shaw

FINDING THE SOURCE

GET BACK IN THE SPACE

Try to write songs that are really meaningful to you, and when you share them with people, make sure you try to get yourself back in that space of when you wrote the song.

—*Jack Johnson*

TRUE MUSIC

There is a great responsibility as a musician to write true music, meaning that it comes from within your soul—something that you truly feel. As a musician, I can't ask for anything more than writing music that will outlive myself.

—*Graham Nash*

THE MUSE

Music is the highest muse.

—*Harry Nilsson*

TIMING

You never can tell when it will happen. You don't have a list of things you're going to invent. It just flashes in your mind.

—*Les Paul*

Harry Nilsson

BEING A GOOD LISTENER

I fill the buckets once a month with new records. Don't copy, but learn from them.

—*Phil Ramone*

INSPIRATION COMES IN ALL FORMS

You hear stories of people who've come from the other side of the tracks and brought inspiration from their upbringing. I think that it's helpful, but at the same time, Cole Porter wrote great songs sipping champagne at a grand piano. Just about anything can work.

—*Robbie Robertson*

Robbie Robertson

FINDING YOUR ROOTS

I think my musical roots are a combination of having some Detroit r&b roots, and then being a little embarrassed being a white Jewish guy imitating it. This is where you get a Bob Dylan, a guy who is essentially half John Lee Hooker and half Jewish intelligentsia. He's the genetic blend of the two.

—*Don Was*

GENIUS

Genius to me speaks very loudly. I heard a definition, once, that genius is making something very complex appear simple.

—*Brian Wilson*

HEARING THINGS

The bummer of being a composer is you sit in the bathtub in the morning, where I do most of my writing, and you hear things in your head. They sound far more 3D and far more wonderful than they will ever sound by the time they make it to the real world.

—Hans Zimmer

Hans Zimmer

IN TUNE WITH THE TIMES

We were pretty much like any other eleven or twelve year old kids, listening to the Rolling Stones. The Mexican music was our parents' music, so we took it for granted. It wasn't until later that we became interested, when we were in high school and the cultural-awareness thing happened in the Mexican-American communities throughout the Southwest. Being musicians, we took on the musical aspect of our culture—something that no one our age was doing anything with.

—David Hidalgo

THE SIXTIES

Robert Heinlein's book, *Stranger in a Strange Land*, provided a model for the Age of Aquarius. People were trying for something that hadn't been done for a while, if ever—particularly in the crucible of sex, drugs, and rock 'n' roll.

—Paul Kantner

Paul Kantner

GETTING INTO YOUR ZONE

If you have an ethnic background, go back and take the best from it, bring it forward, and meld it with good music from the time in which you exist.

—*Taj Mahal*

YOUR PAST LIVES

To come from tradition gives you solidity and a confidence to experiment and explore. If you don't know what the past is, you can't invent the future. To be contemporary and forward looking, you have to know where you came from.

—*Richard Thompson*

BLUEGRASS RELEASE

The music is so happy rhythmically, but ironically, the lyrics may be tragic and sad—stories of the struggle to survive in life. It's a way to confront the negative emotions and the horrific consequences of life's realities, and in a cathartic way purge yourself and find release.

—*Dwight Yoakam*

BODY OF MUSIC

How it connects with the body is the heart and soul of record making.

—*Jon Brion*

Jon Brion

CHOOSING TEACHERS

Baby I Need Your Lovin' was my favorite high school record. I remember looking at the writing credits and thinking, "I don't know who these people are, but I'm going to learn how to write songs from them."

—*Jimmy Webb*

RETURNING TO THE SOURCE

To be inspired, I go back to the things that inspired me to play in the first place—to remind myself why I'm doing this: because I love music. That's why I started playing, before there were girls and money.

—*Steve Lukather*

DRIVING FORCES

THE UNIVERSAL LANGUAGE

I think that music is a universal language, and if someone is singing passionately, then it doesn't matter what part of the globe they are from. They have a very good chance of communicating their feelings very articulately to any listener.

—*Peter Gabriel*

Peter Gabriel

PRIORITIES

The star is still the writer, and the singer is still the most important part of a record.

—*George Martin*

STUDIO ATTITUDE

I talk to the band like this: "We're the young Rolling Stones, we're the young Beatles. We want people to really like us. We're not setting out to be too clever, or too arty, but we love what we're doing, and we want other people to like it, too."

—*Mitchell Froom*

ARTIST ANXIETY

If you have fears, you start to go nuts. It's more about caring and interest than worrying whether you can you do something that you haven't done before.

—*Phil Ramone*

SIMPLICITY

Everything I did was as simple as I could get it, and as reliable and work-able and as stable as possible.

—*Les Paul*

Les Paul

BEATLES WITHOUT BOUNDARIES

They knew how to cut loose without any boundaries. They did whatever the fuck they felt like doing, instead of some sort of formula to get on MTV or something like that. They let it hang out naturally and freely, which is what we try to do.

—*Anthony Kiedis*

CAR TUNES

I do a lot of listening in the car. You can really determine a lot when you are on your way to work.

—*Elliot Scheiner*

RESISTANCE IS VITAL

I'm actually happier when there is some sort of struggle. Most of the people I know in the arts, and in music, feel like that. We need something—a big boulder to push uphill.

—*Walter Becker*

LOVE TO WORK

We work because we love it and the royalties are really a blessing. But without them, we'd still be working. It's just something that we're born to do, so we do it. It's a calling.
—*Booker T. Jones*

IMMERSE YOURSELF

When I was beginning, I was intoxicated with recording. That is all I wanted to do. I lived and breathed it. In the formative years, that kind of obsession is very important.
—*Bruce Botnick*

SLOW PROGRESS

I am lazy, and I work slow, and have high standards that I meander towards.
—*Jackson Browne*

Bruce Botnick

EMOTIONAL RESPONSE

I was never happy in graduate school when we were told to use a system, and approach music like architecture. It's an emotional response, and for me—maybe because I am Italian—music is sourced in the emotions.
—*Suzanne Ciani*

A PURPOSE

I just hope that my music is appreciated by some people as a good thing.
—*Lyle Lovett*

Lyle Lovett

PUZZLE PIECES

My background has been: any elements can be juggled, any elements can be collaged, edited, juxtaposed, to come up with something new.
—*Thomas Dolby*

BEING DANGEROUS

Rock 'n' roll should be dangerous. You're not quite sure what you're getting into. It makes your heart pound a little more. You push yourself past your normal limits and break down the walls that people put up.
—*Paul Kantner*

WORKING WITH GENIUS

Jimi would come up with new sounds—do things that left us breathless. That would inspire us to be different, take a chance, mic it in a different way, EQ in a new way—whatever was needed to take his ideas to another level.
—*Eddie Kramer*

BEYOND HIT RECORDS

With an artist like Eric Clapton, you almost have to forget about getting a hit record, because he's very pure in his point of view.
—*Russ Titelman*

Russ Titelman

CELEBRATE YOUR DIFFERENCE

I knew that what I was going to do would be different, and I didn't want to do what everyone else did. I wasn't going to straighten my hair and wear sequined suits and ignore my culture. Nor was I going to make my culture better by putting down someone else's.
—*Taj Mahal*

BORN TO PLAY

I've had this thing in my head since I was in high school that maybe someday I would actually have to get a real job and go into another line of work. I don't take it for granted that I will always be doing this, but I can't imagine what the hell else I would be doing.

—*Michael McDonald*

DISCOVERING THE STUDIO

When I was at school, I read science subjects and was also very interested in music. The amalgamation of the two equaled the recording studio. When I first saw a copy of *Studio Sound* and the consoles with all the knobs, I thought, "That's the life for me."

—*Hugh Padgham*

Hugh Padgham

SURROUND YOURSELF WITH TALENT

Whenever young guys ask me what they should do to get better, I always say, try to be the worst guy in whatever band you're in. That's the secret.

—*Pat Metheny*

HE'S A REBEL

I am an entrepreneur at heart, and a rebel. If somebody says this is the normal way of doing it, I want to find another way.

—*Rupert Neve*

Rupert Neve

THE BIG BREAK

SLEEP IS NOT ALWAYS AN OPTION

I had been up late in some clubs, and at seven o'clock in the morning, I get this phone call. "Hi, this is Frank Zappa. I'm looking for a keyboard player. Want to audition?" I said, "Yes, of course! When?" And he said, "Now." So, at seven in the morning, I got in my car and drove up to his home, and I auditioned the entire day.
—*Peter Wolf*

OVERCOMING FEAR

I had just gone to work for a publishing company. My publisher said to me, "I've got a song title for you, "Me and Bobby McGee," but here's the hook—Bobby is a she." I'm thinking, holy shit, I can't do this.
—*Kris Kristofferson*

Kris Kristofferson

IT COULD HAPPEN

With all the people I knew who were working around L.A., I thought somebody would quit, or drop out of a band, and they would think of me. But other than fantasizing, I didn't seriously think it would happen.
—*Michael McDonald*

SEIZE THE MOMENT

I started in 1959 at RCA recording studios in Nashville. Chet Atkins, who was in charge, was a very mild-mannered person, but for some reason, he had just had a fight and punched out the engineer. I learned there was an immediate job opening and went for it.

—Bill Porter

AUDITIONING FOR THE E STREET BAND

I saw the ad: "Wanted: Drummer. No junior Ginger Bakers." This imme-diately told me that he wanted an accompanist, so I just brought a bass drum, a snare drum, hi-hat, and cymbal to the audition. As it turned out, it was one of the most impressive things I could have done, because the guy who auditioned before me came in with six toms, eight cymbals, big set of drums, and played like Carmine Appice. He could play, but it wasn't what they wanted. I sat down to play and immediately it felt right—from the first note.

Max Weinberg

—Max Weinberg

ARRANGING THE WALL OF SOUND

I was in a building on Sunset that had a lot of music people in it. Lester Sill was a floor above me, and one day came down and said Phil Spector was in town and was looking for an arranger. I met him, and he played the demo for "He's a Rebel." We became friends and worked together from then on.

—Jack Nitzsche

THAT FIRST CHECK

The first royalty check I ever got was from a Supremes Christmas album—$350 for a song called "My Christmas Tree." It had never occurred to me before that I could make money doing this; I had always been doing it for fun.

—*Jimmy Webb*

CREATING RESULTS

IN THE NOW

You tend to get the most done in the moment—if you stick with it. People are into the real feeling of a track when they're doing it, not coming back to it later, trying to remember.
—*Mitchell Froom*

Mitchell Froom

NEED FOR RENEWAL

People have to understand that when you play the same song over and over again for twenty years, you might get sick of that song. It's great when you can come up with a new arrangement, because it's like doing a new song.
—*Al Kooper*

CREATIVE PROCESSING

You create by trying things out and listening, reacting, and changing your ideas. There develops a pattern match—the more difficult the idea, the more extreme the tangents.
—*George Massenburg*

THE HITCHCOCK STRATEGY

I'm loath to go into something if I can't hear it first. It's like Hitchcock used to do elaborate planning. I don't have to hear every guitar part beforehand, but if I can't imagine what the overall texture will be, I figure I have nothing to offer.

—*Don Was*

BE OF SERVICE

When you're scoring, your job is to serve the film. The second job is make your lead actors look wonderful. Support them, because then your film will be better.

—*Hans Zimmer*

HAVE A PLAN

It's very easy to get lost in the technology. You have so many choices that if you don't have an initial idea of how you want to work, you'll spend all your time wandering around in the wilderness of possibilities.

—*Walter Becker*

Walter Becker

DON'T ASSUME

An assumption is the mother of a fuckup.

—*Artie Shaw*

BE READY, HAVE BACKUP

In Sinatra's case, a lot of times, he would do one take and say, "That's it—I'm never gonna sing it any better." Can you imagine asking *him* if he could sing it again? I got to the point where I learned that the minute he walked in, you would record everything—the rehearsal, a guy warming up in the corner. You might need one note to edit in somewhere.

—*Lee Herschberg*

CAN DO

Don't listen to people who tell you what you can and cannot do, or should or shouldn't use. It's wide open. You can use just about anything to record everything and should.
—*Tchad Blake*

LESS IS MORE

Van Morrison taught me the power of simplicity—that if you pick the right notes, it only takes a few of them. He's the master of that.
—*Mark Isham*

Tchad Blake

GETTING THE SOUND

Certain artists say they don't like effects; they want an organic natural sound. If they can hear the effect, then it is too much. But if it's tucked in subtly, and it adds dimension, then they are more willing to accept it and enjoy it.
—*Kevin Killen*

YOU'RE A TOUGH ACT TO FOLLOW

With many artists who do their own songs, the best record is the first one, because they have five to ten years of material they've collected. For the next album, you go to the B catalog, or you have to write it all in that year.
—*Michael McDonald*

MENTAL NOTES

I get a concept when I hear a song. Almost immediately, I have a feeling of where I am going to put delays or reverb. I just get a vibe and keep fiddling around until it equals what I'm thinking in my head.
—*Hugh Padgham*

STEELY DAN TIME

I had never worked on any record that long. I would get a mix and think it was great, and they'd want the guitar up in one spot. We'd get that and then they would want something else. It went on and on, but it did get better and better, and when we finished we had great records.

—Al Schmitt

Al Schmitt

THE SELECTION OPTION

I was under the impression that "creation" of music is all there is. After working with Tangerine Dream, I began to see "selection" as the other complementary principle to coming up with something, and one that is becoming even more important as we are flooded with options by advances in technology. There is a skill in selecting that one moment that is actually worth something.

—Paul Haslinger

TRANSCENDING

I want to be able to get lost in what I am hearing, and when the music starts, I am in that place until the song has ended. I am both lost, and getting little gifts as the song goes along. I'm looking for that transcendent experience.

—Jon Brion

THE HUMAN TOUCH

We have moved into an age of sophisticated sound. With digital recording, everything must be perfect. But you still must have the feeling of a human presence in the music.

—*Maurice Jarre*

Maurice Jarre

HARD TO BE SIMPLE

I think that the simplicity of an image or of a sound is hard to make. It means the artist has to throw a lot away, and just use the most important and the strongest things.

—*Laurie Anderson*

GETTING SESSION WORK

You have to be where the business is. Next step, people have to know you; you have to get out and play, get a reputation. And never give up. As soon as you put the instrument in the corner, it's all over.

—*Tommy Tedesco*

Tommy Tedesco

IMPROVISATION

GOING WHERE YOU'VE NEVER BEEN

What I am talking about in my music is the attempt to get into a state of improvisation every night. That means you start out with things you know—patterns and techniques that you've learned over the years—and you try to go from those into areas where you've never been before.

—*Mose Allison*

COLOR OUTSIDE THE LINES

When you read music, there is a part of your brain that shuts down. It's like coloring within the lines. You don't take off. What a coloring book does is completely kill creativity.

—*David Lynch*

David Lynch

SURF MUSIC

Surfing has helped me in learning how to improvise. It's like riding a wave. You never really know what the wave is going to be like. You gotta change and make split-second decisions.

—*Jack Johnson*

NO RULES

One time, we put a prophylactic on a long thin mic, put it into a milk bottle filled with water and then put headsets on the bottle to send a sound through. Basically, what the guys at A&R Studios taught me was that anything goes. Don't be afraid. There are no rules—no holds barred in getting sounds. You have to go out there and work your ass off to make it sound exciting.

—*Shelly Yakus*

Shelly Yakus

GET OUT OF THE CORNER

It was decided that for the first time, for *Voodoo Lounge*, the Rolling Stones were going to plan the album before they started recording. There were no songs written yet, and all of a sudden I get this fax from Keith: "Be in Dublin next week to start the album." I faxed him back that I thought we were going to plan it all out first. What are we doing? He faxed back and said: "That's for me to know and you to find out. When you get to Dublin: improvise, adapt, overcome, and p-fucking-s, don't paint yourself into a corner."

—*Don Was*

FIND YOUR EDGE

Be an innovator and not a follower. Don't be afraid to step away from what everybody else is doing. Satisfy yourself.

—*Steve Lukather*

Steve Lukather

COLLABORATION

TWO FOR ONE

When you are writing with someone, you not only have a partner—you have an audience for your ideas.

—*Walter Becker*

ARTIST/PRODUCER RELATIONSHIP

For me, the most important thing is the motivation of the artist and the commitment to making great music. That is the first question: What do you want to do?

—*Glen Ballard*

Glen Ballard

GOOD COMPANY

I've always felt that I was in partnership with the record company, and if I could discover something wrong in the manufacturing, we should work together to make a better product when it is not cost prohibitive. Usually, it only takes caring to correct the deficiencies.

—*Tim Weisberg*

WORKING IT OUT

If I am working alone and I don't like an idea, I am free to throw it away and go on. When you're co-writing, you can get boxed in a little, because out of common courtesy, you can't just blow somebody off in the middle of a song and say, "I don't feel like working on this anymore."

—*Michael McDonald*

COLLABORATING WITH GENIUS

Otis Redding always had more ideas than any writer I ever worked with. We wrote "Dock of the Bay" in the studio. He had an intro and that first little verse about watching the ships come in and watchin' 'em roll away again. He was humming a little melody, and I sat there and finished the lyrics with him and wrote the bridge to it.

—*Steve Cropper*

Steve Cropper

PART OF THE PICTURE

Maybe because I was trained in the theater, I see music as part of the whole—a collaboration. If you are doing music for film, you must understand that your music won't be up front; it's counterpoint.

—*Maurice Jarre*

CHECK THE EGO

There's no way to collaborate unless the two people are willing to let go of an awful lot of ego and pride. All that has to go out the window.

—*Jimmy Webb*

KEEPING YOUR INTEGRITY

DUE DILIGENCE
Paying the dues is learning how to believe in yourself, when all the evidence is to the contrary.
—*Kris Kristofferson*

HITS THE TRUTH
Be true to the song. If everything is honest, there's a chance it will work. The "hit" comes after the fact.
—*Phil Ramone*

Phil Ramone

ATTITUDE
It's only when you're in a humble place that you really have the opportunity to be a hero.
—*Robbie Robertson*

NO REGRETS
The most important thing to me has always been to satisfy myself, and therefore, I can't really have a lot of regrets. And I really don't blame anyone else for the way my life has turned out.
—*Todd Rundgren*

STAND BEHIND IT

I want people to come in to my studio and make music that is the truth and something they can stand behind and put out into the world.
—*Linda Perry*

AT YOUR BEST

If you are playing honestly, you are at the edge of your ability—and you are pushing at that, trying to go farther.
—*Artie Shaw*

Linda Perry

BUCKING THE TREND

The people who are inspirational to me are guys who don't care if they are trendy or not—the ones who have defied categorization. They do a body of work. Some things are better than others, but if you are looking for a 25-year run, you better lift yourself out of this trend thing or you go down with it.
—*Don Was*

Don Was

TRUST FUND

Always earn the trust of the record buyer.
—*Will Ackerman*

LASTING IMPRESSIONS

I just want to do good work and hopefully be outside time and fashion.
—*Tchad Blake*

GOOD CREATION

When you make something that satisfies your own integrity, what you feel is good creation. It goes out there into the world and has an impact on people, and hopefully enriches their lives. As a group of human beings, for a moment, things are a little better.

—*Mark Isham*

Mark Isham

SPEAK UP

We took the route that has ultimately been more difficult: to make music that we feel really says something, and is different, and doesn't sacrifice our integrity, our culture, and our ethnic background.

—*Louie Perez*

THE MAGIC

GOOSE BUMPS

I'm a musician to the core. I wake up in the morning thinking about music, and usually sit down at the piano and fool around with chords and try to write a song. I'm looking for that rush—that goose bump experience that now and then comes when you hit that right sequence of chords.
—*Herb Alpert*

Herb Alpert

QUANTUM MUSIC THEORY

Sometimes you start a set out, and for no reason that you can figure out or predict, everything starts clicking right away. It's as if it's happening of its own accord. You have control, but you are not forcing anything. I call it the "Spime," my word for space-time. When you get into the Spime, that's when you feel the flow of things, and there is no effort involved. It just happens.
—*Mose Allison*

MICK'S TRICKS

Mick Jagger just kills me. He sings a song, and it's sexy, it's on the money, he sells the emotion. When he gets in front of a microphone, strange magic happens.

—*Ed Cherney*

ROY HAD IT

I remember watching Roy Orbison play live and thinking he makes it look so damn easy. The guy had so much talent that there was really no need for him to "entertain" except for singing these songs he'd written. The most moving performance I ever saw.

—*Chris Isaak*

PROOF OF LIFE

I can tell if the piece is alive, if the performance is alive—as opposed to studied, or desperate, or overthought, or underthought.

—*Leo Kottke*

Leo Kottke

WHOLE LOT O' SERENDIPITY

Track 8 was the final vocal, and 7 was the one prior. For some reason, 7 was breaking through the console, and I couldn't turn it off, so you could hear it, "Wo-man . . . you . . . need . . . it," slightly out of time, so I just cranked up the reverb, and Page heard it and said, "Great, just leave it!"

—*Eddie Kramer*

IS IT A HIT?

When you're confronted with a song like "Every Breath You Take," you know it's a hit before you even start moving a fader up.

—*Hugh Padgham*

FINISHING THE MIX

There's a point that just clicks in and you know when it works. Instinctively, there is that point.

—*Mike Shipley*

Mike Shipley

3

CAREERS

GETTING IT TOGETHER

PAWNSHOP GUITAR

In the sixties, my mother bought me a pawnshop guitar, and I was off and running. It was a way to meet girls, and it sort of raised me above the crowd. Ultimately, it saved us from getting involved in gangs.

—Louie Perez

FINDING WORK

There are only so many jobs out there. You have to get going any way you can, by stringing together stuff at home, or going out on the road with somebody. Determination will always win out.

—Alan Parsons

THE FIRST BREAK

Nashville saved my life. I deliberately went in at the bottom, to learn about recording studios from the bottom up. The position I found was very easy to fit into: janitor at a recording studio. Billy Swan got it for me. He had the job before me and wanted to quit. I guess the stress was too much.

—Kris Kristofferson

Kris Kristofferson

BRAINERCISE

You have to stretch your mind. It's like a green animal skin. If you don't learn new things, and you don't play all the time, it contracts, and gets hard and inflexible.

—*David Lindley*

FOR THE RECORD

Rather than going out on stage and doing big guitar solos, I wanted more to make the whole thing come together—write it, produce it, play guitar, and then make it into a record. That was the biggest thrill: to make a record.

—*Jeff Lynne*

UNIQUENESS

I am always searching for artists who have their own unique point of view, sound, and vision.

—*Joe Chiccarelli*

Joe Chiccarelli

CAREER LONGEVITY

In the pop world, you quite rapidly become obsolete and useless. But in the classical and jazz worlds, there is longevity, and people think in terms of longer careers.

—*Tim Weisberg*

IT'S A LIVING

I didn't consciously make a decision to be a musician. I was musical as a child—wrote songs and sang them in grade school. It's always meant a lot to me, but I never did sit down and say, "That's what I want to be." I just figured that as long as I could make a living with music, I would do it. When club owners ask what they should say before the show, I tell them, "Here's a man who is in his forty-second year of on-the-job training."

—*Mose Allison*

Mose Allison

TAKING IT ON THE ROAD

THE FUN FACTOR

Going on the road and playing gigs is definitely the most fun you can possibly have. You get this sense of immediate accomplishment, as opposed to sitting around in the studio wondering if there's enough reverb on the snare drum.

—*Pat Metheny*

WARMING UP

Before the show, I have to tune my guitar, so I figure I also have to tune myself. In ten minutes, I try as best as I can, before we go on, to hand over my expectations and speculations of how the show should run or what it should sound like, and receive what it is going to be, because it's never like you planned anyway.

—*Carlos Santana*

Carlos Santana

THE OPENING NUMBER

For the beginning of the show, I like to meditate and ring bells to connect with the audience. Inside the sounds of the bell is a sonic texture that is good for meditation, and I am using that sound with my music to create an experience that I hope is worthwhile.

—*Kitaro*

ANOTHER FIRST SHOW

When we tour, the only difference each night is the audience. It might be your eightieth show, but it is the audience's first, and you play it like the first show.
—*Leland Sklar*

RECREATOR

Tours are a chance of actually recreating some of the magical emotions you have already had—but doing them live and sharing those emotions as best you can with people.
—*Stevie Wonder*

WHEN IT ALL COMES TOGETHER

Stevie Wonder

There have been a couple of times at the club where you could feel the air change. The people would feed the band, and we would play better and better. It goes back and forth, like sex. That's the big exchange, the one that really matters.
—*David Lindley*

STAGE SWEAT

I get drenched on stage. I work out on stage, not running around, but I put everything I have into every note.
—*Duane Eddy*

TOUGH LOVE

Frank Zappa was a strict disciplinarian. If it was wrong, even in performance, he would make you do it again. I had it happen, once. He stopped the band, and said, "Stop. George made a mistake. Do it again." It was embarrassing, and the crowd all laughed, but Frank was serious. I said to myself, I would never let that happen to me again.

—*George Duke*

George Duke

KNOW THE SCORE

Toscanini was the one who started the fad of conducting without a score, but that was a need for him. He was very myopic, and he once told me, "You know, I can't conduct looking at the score close up like this." So he said, "The hell with it. I gotta learn it, that's all. I want to look at the orchestra." And all the other conductors imitated that afterwards.

—*Carmine Coppola*

WHERE TO FOCUS

Singing on stage, I try to focus on the emotion that was the catalyst for the song.

—*Dwight Yoakam*

CONDUCTING ELECTRICITY

It occurred to me when I was fourteen that the guy who mixed the sound at rock concerts was like a twentieth century conductor. Moving the faders was like using the baton, and he was the interface between the musicians and the audience.

—*David Tickle*

David Tickle

DAMAGE CONTROL

The night of our first show at Madison Square Garden, our first arena gig, my bass drum skin snaps. When you break a tom-tom or snare drum skin, it's easy. Pull it off, throw on your spare. But when your bass drum skin goes, you have to stop the show, pull off a forest of microphones, take away all the other drums to get to the bass drum beneath everything. It's like having to remove the engine from a car. Fifty roadies jumped out of the wings and leapt upon the task while the three of us were standing on the stage and telling jokes. We made a big deal of it, and it actually warmed the place up. When it was done and we went back and kicked in the first note, the place went ape crazy. The lesson is: any adversity that strikes while you are on stage can be turned to your advantage.

—*Stewart Copeland*

THE ROOM SOUND

There are such a variety of factors in live recording. Most amazing to me is the sound of the room, which affects everything. Sometimes, you think you can just replace the ambience, but many of these concert halls have an ambience that is very potent in the mic.

—*Jackson Browne*

JUST KIDDIN'

Usually, when I forget the lyrics, I just pretend to mouth the words for a few seconds, then I tap the microphone a couple times and glare angrily at the sound engineer.

—"Weird Al" Yankovic

"Weird Al" Yankovic

IN THE STUDIO

USE TIME WISELY

You can spend ninety percent of your time worrying over something that is only worth ten percent. Prioritizing how you spend time is probably the biggest thing I can bring to the entire process of recording.
—*Glen Ballard*

CREATIVE WORKS

Making records is supposed to be a creative working environment. Most of us do this because we didn't want typical jobs that mirrored the way society works.
—*Jon Brion*

TIGHTEN UP

I believe there has to be a certain amount of tension in order to get the best work out of everyone.
—*David Foster*

DIAL IT UP

Don't get hung up on the technology. They really make it easy for you nowadays. It's just a matter of pushing buttons, and turning the knobs until it sounds right.
—*Bob Clearmountain*

David Foster

Q'S APPROACH

Quincy has a kaleidoscopic approach to music, examining it from one angle, then turning it and looking from another angle.
—*Bruce Swedien*

NO FEAR

It's important to learn the gear so that when you want to create something, you're not stuck having to translate the idea to somebody else. And this goes for women, especially. You can't be afraid of the technology.
—*Wendy Melvoin*

FEEL THE BEAT

In a great many records made by hit artists, the drums play a huge part in

Wendy Melvoin

whether they become hits, because of the way it feels when it comes over that little speaker. Generally, the first thing that a person feels is the way the drummer has constructed the heartbeat of the song.
—*Jim Keltner*

PRODUCING

THE RESPONSIBILITY

I am the first person to hear what this artist has to say, and how they are going to say it. It's like a sacred Hippocratic oath: to first do no harm, but really be involved.

—*Glen Ballard*

HARNESSING THE ENERGY

The producer keeps a balance between work and relaxing, and maintains complete clarity and focus. He keeps his objectivity while we are completely caught up and emotional. We're just exploding and coming up with all kinds of stuff, and he helps us harness our energy.

—*Flea*

Flea

DREAM PRODUCER

The best producer is someone who is a fan. You can hear it in your head. I used to dream the next Bob Dylan album, the next Beatles album. I wish I could have woken up and written down the songs. I dreamt whole Beatles songs that never existed, because I was so excited about what was coming next.

—*Don Was*

THE ROLES OF PRODUCERS AND ENGINEERS

I'm the old-fashioned type of producer who likes to work with an engineer. I think the two roles are very difficult to combine. I feel that the guy who concentrates on the art, the production, and the music shouldn't really be bothered with whether the microphone is on the blink or not, or whether the EQ switch is dirty.

—*George Martin*

PRESERVING THE INTENTION

It's not only that my producer, Jon Brion, wants to make a good record. He wants to make the record that the songwriter intended. He knows that I will be going out to play this.

—*Fiona Apple*

Fiona Apple

MEETING MY NEEDS

My main criterion is for a producer to provide camaraderie, more than a technical expertise. I want them to relate to the work, to dig it, and help to bring an atmosphere of confidence.

—*Rickie Lee Jones*

GETTING BACK ON TRACK

Every time we started recording the next Billy Joel album, we asked, "How do we get the motors going?" That's what a good producer is supposed to know: how to get that motor going for everybody.

—*Phil Ramone*

PRODUCERS' SENSITIVITY

You have to be a good babysitter/ psychologist. The artist can get sidetracked and discouraged, and you must be sensitive and nonthreatening, while pushing them to top themselves.

—*Geza X*

Geza X

LEARNING FROM PHIL

I learned from Phil Spector how to make "Wouldn't It Be Nice." I learned "Good Vibrations" from "Da Doo Ron Ron." And I learned from him to get farther into what I'm doing and then force it in the positive direction, rather than just sit around and think about it. I figured, if he could do it, I could do it. Using a little extra effort makes the difference on the whole damn thing.

—*Brian Wilson*

A MATTER OF TASTE

Most of production is taste, and you try not to get too much of yourself into it. What we are supposed to do is recognize raw talent, and to understand how to pull all the elements together to achieve in the final product what was precious to begin with. Enhance and support, and you end up with the best of the artist.

—*David Kershenbaum*

JOB REQUIREMENTS

What makes a great producer? Patience, tenacity, and a degree in psychology.

—*Eddie Kramer*

PART CHAMELEON

A producer is a lot of things—an editor, an objective ear. It's also being a casting director, choosing who to bring in to play. It depends on what's going on. Sometimes you're an arranger, sometimes you just back off and are there to be a support.

—*Russ Titelman*

IT'S NOT MY EGO

I don't want to have my stamp on a record; I want to help the artist get their essence recorded well. The music producer is like a film director. You are a motivator, and hopefully, a big-picture person, and you most of all want the artist to feel comfortable in order to yield the best results.

—*John Alagia*

John Alagia

TRUST THEM

A great producer is like a great director in motion pictures. He or she knows how to cast the work at hand, choose the right musicians, engineers, orchestrators, copyists, and then give them the freedom to do what they do well.

—*Bruce Swedien*

PRODUCER CHOPS

A great producer is one who is musically aware, totally in touch with the artist's vision, and at the same time, able to tactfully take control when necessary. He or she must also be a motivated businessperson who has the personality and confidence to reassure the people who are putting up the big bucks for the record.
—*James West*

James West

ARCHITECTING MUSIC

I see music architecturally, as a spatial thing—left to right, front to back, up and down. It's animated, and it's moving in real time. Kanye West has that. He tries things out until it all fits—until it sits where it is supposed to sit, and everything has the correct emotional function.
—*Jon Brion*

STUDIO THERAPY

The artist may have a block of some kind, and your job is to help them get past it. It's a constant process to get something out of another human being. I think the really great producers are all master psychologists.
—*Jimmy Webb*

PREREQUISITES

Some producers are arrangers. Some producers are mixers. Some are songwriters, musicians, or artists themselves. The best ones don't try to be what they're not.
—*Bob Clearmountain*

Bob Clearmountain

SONGWRITING

MAKE IT FUN

If you can combine a great song and a great artist, and make it fun
to listen to—you've got it. A lot of the big records over the years have
been fun to listen to.

—*Herb Alpert*

THE GOOD SONG

Good songwriting is the best pre-production in the world. Good songs
are pretty much indestructible. A good song badly produced is still a
good song.

—*Jon Brion*

MY STARTING POINT

I usually start humming, or making
sounds, and then I find the melody,
and then the melody sets a mood
for me, and there might be a certain
word that just fits in the melody. And
the song starts growing from that
word.

—*Jack Johnson*

Jack Johnson

PETER GUNN

It's an anthem. We all like to write anthems, and I've had a couple. Just take the bass figure. You've got six or seven notes there and it never changes during the whole piece. Any kid playing guitar can pick that out, and look real good if he plays bass with the band. The melody is very simple—only one chord in the whole piece.

—*Henry Mancini*

MUSICAL ALCHEMY

As artists, we've always wanted to be our own psychiatrists in a way. We have the ability, because we are writers, to internalize situations and then bring them out as music.

—*Graham Nash*

THE MOST IMPORTANT THING

The most important thing is the song. If you have a great song, there is a whole lot of slack you get everywhere else. The performance doesn't have to be perfect—it just has to be sympathetic to the song.

—*Todd Rundgren*

Todd Rundgren

MAKE THE MOST OF IT

I think it's easier to write when you're devastated. Love songs can be really sappy when you're deeply in love and you've lost focus. Sorrow, despair, and desperation lend themselves to a much better song.

—*Jann Arden*

IN THE MIDNIGHT HOUR

If you go back and listen to the stuff Wilson Pickett sang in the late fifties and early sixties, he goes into these fade-outs with "I'm Gonna See My Jesus in the Midnight Hour." It was sort of his identity, and that's where I got the idea for the song. Of course, he jumped right on it, and we wrote that song in about an hour.

—Steve Cropper

THE WRITER'S LOT

I liked the idea of the scribe, and I liked folk music a lot—ideas, words, and truths filtering from generation to generation, turned this way and that.

—Jackson Browne

ROY ORBISON SAID

Always have a little bit of hope in your songs.

—Chris Isaak

Chris Isaak

TELL IT LIKE IT IS

I don't make great differentiations among styles of music. It's all just music to me. Whether you are orchestrating a soundtrack or writing a pop song, you are trying to tell a story, musically and lyrically.

—Glen Ballard

SURPRISE!

With every song, you are trying to find a moment that completely surprises you. A song doesn't come to life until something happens in that song that you could never possibly have thought of.

—*Tom McRae*

Tom McRae

PRESS AND RELEASE

In all music, the establishment of tension, and then the release of tension, is important. In Bruce's music, it's critical.

—*Max Weinberg*

A LIFE OF ITS OWN

At times, you have to forget your pride and your ego to make the song work. As you develop the song, it takes on its own characteristics and becomes what's good for *it*. Your idea gets mutated.

—*Fee Waybill*

IT'S NOT OVER 'TIL IT'S OVER

I revise my lyrics, even years later. I say, don't ever put 'em away until you really have to—until you've got a major artist recording it. Until then, you can keep making it better.

—*Jimmy Webb*

MOTOWN'S FORMULA

We wanted to have the type of music that would appeal to both black and white. It didn't really affect our writing; it affected our judgment. We knew that whites were into a more melodic type of music, but the blacks liked rhythm. So we tried a combination.

—*Brian Holland*

Brian Holland

ENGINEERING

THE RIGHT TOOLS

My job is to create an environment to capture musical moments and convert them into a listenable product. To reach that goal, I will use whatever equipment or tricks I know.
—*Dave Reitzas*

Dave Reitzas

STAND UP

Purely as an engineer, you must have very little ego, because you are dealing with big enough egos as it is and another one just doesn't help. As an engineer/producer, you have to be a little more forceful and stand up for what you think.
—*Eddy Offord*

THE SKILL SET

I remember Geoff Emerick's ability to set up a board before a session, before anybody had arrived, and then to push up the faders on the downbeat and everything would be there. I feel that to be a true pro engineer, you should be able to anticipate what levels to expect out of what mics, how to record them, and what EQ they are going to need.
—*Alan Parsons*

WORKING WITH MY ENGINEER

Ed Cherney taught me that if you are thinking of an effect, then go ahead and try it. It only takes four minutes. He doesn't like talking about things; he likes to try them.

—*Jann Arden*

WORK THE ROOM

Basically, I am an acoustical engineer. I like working with orchestras, and the more players there are, the happier I am. I try to be in the studio, listen to what it sounds like in there, and then do my best to capture that.

—*Al Schmitt*

WHAT I WANT FROM AN ENGINEER

Someone who can work really fast. The worst thing for a musician is to sit around waiting for machines. It just kills the creativity. I want to walk in and play, and be engaged in my process.

—*Andy Summers*

Andy Summers

AND WHAT I WANT

Quickness, attention, ability, agility, intelligence, and commitment to a project.

—*Steve Miller*

HOOKED ON ENGINEERING

I don't like producing. I've been asked quite often to produce, and people are surprised when I turn them down. I just feel that I am a better engineer than I am a producer. I like helping people make their records.

—*Shelly Yakus*

GOOD ENGINEERING

A good engineer thinks like a musician as much as an engineer, and everything he or she does is designed to help the song and the total situation.

—*Danny Kortchmar*

Danny Kortchmar

MY FIRST BEATLES ALBUM

Revolver was the first album I engineered. It was, "Well, Geoff's the engineer. We don't want the piano to sound like a piano. We don't want the guitar to sound like a guitar, and we don't want the drums to sound like drums." This was mainly coming from Lennon.

—*Geoff Emerick*

GOFER INITIATIVE

As an assistant, you must be very patient and understand that in order to lead, you must learn how to serve. My role as an assistant was to operate the tape machine, shut up, and try to second guess what the engineer and producer might want. Anticipate. Take some initiative. If they are about to run out of coffee, don't ask, just get it.

—*Ralph Sutton*

STUDIO MUSICIANS

SESSION PLAYERS

In the seventies, everybody got hip to what a studio musician was. You heard about people who played on everyone's records. To be in the Muscle Shoals Rhythm Section was happening. I thought, "Boy, that's what I want to be."
—*Paul Shaffer*

SESSION CAT WORK ETHIC

I have pride about my job as a profession. When they are doing playbacks, I don't sit around with my cell phone, bullshitting. I go in and listen to the playback and become involved. It's more than, "I played my part and I'm done." Work on getting a good sound; don't expect the engineer to do everything for you. If my name is going to be on it, I want it to be the best it can be—to be proud of it.
—*Leland Sklar*

Leland Sklar

JUST LET 'EM PLAY

When you are asking great musicians to contribute, you don't want to tell them what to play.
—*Graham Nash*

GUARANTEED GOLD

It made the sessions particularly exciting and rewarding when we were working with Phil Spector or Brian Wilson, because we knew we were making hit records. They just had an edge over everything else.
—*Steve Douglas*

Graham Nash

KEEP IT UP

When studio musicians have done so many sessions that it's just another date in the book, another job, then they are no longer a help on the record. So much of it has to do with keeping the enthusiasm.
—*Jack Nitzsche*

THE MASKED GUITAR SLINGER

They'd call me in as a guitar player, and I would look at the booth, and it was completely blank to me. The singers, too. Now, I look back, and it's hysterical to find out about all the people I worked with. I didn't realize all the hits I made. At the time, it didn't mean a thing; I was just a dedicated studio guitar player.
—*Tommy Tedesco*

LENNON SESSIONS

The big difference between working with John and a lot of other people was that his songs played themselves. They were just so complete when he came to us with them that there was hardly ever any reworking. It all just fell into place.

—*Jim Keltner*

Jim Keltner

SCORING

MOVIE MUSIC
Basically, the idea is to get the music on the film and have it make some sort of sense. The quest is always the same.
—*Henry Mancini*

WHO'S THE BOSS?
I don't work for the director or the producer. I work for the film, just as the director does. You hang on for dear life, and the film is dictating what it requires.
—*Hans Zimmer*

CAN YOU HUM IT?
The public would like to leave the movie humming a tune. That's a test of simplicity.
—*Carmine Coppola*

Carmine Coppola

ENHANCE THE EXPERIENCE

I think watching a movie should be an experience. The music's most important role is to enhance—in some cases, even to establish that experience. To do that, a composer needs to understand the history and craft of storytelling and its application in film. And you must understand psychological effect.

—Paul Haslinger

STAY ON STORY

If we do our job exceptionally well, nobody notices. Because what they hear matches what they see. They take it for granted. But if you don't pull it off, the sound can take you out of the story.

—John Neff

COMPOSING ELECTRONICALLY

John Neff

Electronic instruments are great for the composer. I understand the musician's argument, but the virtuosos and the great musicians will always be here. Electronics can't do everything, but it does eliminate the unconcerned attitudes that some musicians have.

—Jack Nitzsche

COUNTERPOINT

I try to create rhythmic oppositions between music and images—a counterpoint. I think people are capable of absorbing a lot of time signatures simultaneously.

—Laurie Anderson

ALEATORICISM EXPLAINED

Bartók was the first guy to say, "Let's never repeat a note or musical phrase." The next logical idea after that was, hey, let's not play notes, let's play something random. That's basically what aleatoricism is: introducing randomization into a composition. You give the players a motif or a theme, or a range you want them to play in. Oftentimes, the notation for

Brian "BT" Transeau

the cue will be longer than the musical notes you write. It's fun to do in films, and it's very wild. It makes hideous, ugly, scary music—an incredible sound, when you get it right.

—*Brian "BT" Transeau*

COMPOSING ON THE PIANO

For composing music for film, I like the piano. It's a very beautiful instrument, and it's convenient to write on top of it.

—*Maurice Jarre*

KEYS TO SUCCESS

DIG YOUR GIG

The key to my success is the fact that I will get to play again this week. I like playing, and I like what I'm doing. I'm fortunate. Throughout my career, I've run across super-talented people all over the world—and you'll never hear of them. They were never able to make a living, or they gave it up. I've kept at it, and no matter how sentimental and silly it is, I still keep trying to do a good job.

—*Mose Allison*

IT AIN'T GETTING ANY EASIER

I think it will be very difficult in the future for an artist to sustain a long career. It will be much more of a song-by-song business, and that will make it much harder to break career artists. It will be more expensive. But there will always be artists who defy these changes—who come in off the street with a track they made at home that can change the world.

—*Ron Fair*

Ron Fair

LEADERSHIP STYLES

There are two styles: intimidation and collaboration. I much prefer the collaboration approach, and I am always trying to direct it toward the goal of communicating as clearly and as powerfully as possible.
—*Glen Ballard*

DEDICATION

If you are absolutely one-hundred percent convinced that you want to be a musician or songwriter, and are willing to devote your whole life to it, not get sidetracked, and are prepared to work sixteen hours a day, then you might make it. That's what it takes. Nothing less will do.
—*David Foster*

ILLUSIONS

The whole idea is creating an illusion—taking the spark and making it come alive for a listener sitting at home in Davenport, Iowa.
—*George Massenburg*

GO FOR IT

Do one thing really, really well.
—*Mark Mothersbaugh*

MUSICAL CHEERS

Anyone who wants to know how to do a musical should go see *The Umbrellas of Cherbourg*. It's pure opera from beginning to end and yet any nine year old can enjoy it. It's not arty or over the heads of people, and there is one glorious melody after another.
—*Steve Allen*

Steve Allen

GET OUT OF YOUR WAY

You just have to believe that it is going to happen. Fortunately, we are not in control. If you get out of the way and let it happen, most of the time, it will. We get in our own way more than anybody else does.
—*Willie Nelson*

BECOME A GENIUS

A genius does things most people don't even think of—things there is no accounting for. I know five simple steps to becoming a genius. (1) Find yourself a genius. (2) Make friends with them. (3) Follow them around. (4) Watch what they do. (5) Do it. It might take you thirty years, and you might not become one, but you'll learn something about what it takes.
—*Artie Shaw*

HANG IN THERE

I respect and admire those artists who never give up, no matter how many times people suggest they do.
—*David St. Hubbins*

CIRCLE OF SUCCESS

Surround yourself with great people, and you can't go wrong.
—*C.J. Vanston*

C.J. Vanston

HOLES IN THE WHOLE

You've got to see the forest and not examine each tree. If you find a good song and sing it well, people will respond to it. You can get lost in the digital delays and all the other stuff. It's important to learn restraint. People talk about Sonny Rollins and how the spaces are as important as the notes. It's the same when you produce records. The holes in there can make your point.

—*Don Was*

NO SLEEPING ON THE JOB

Practice, practice, practice! I don't want any of you having to sleep your way to the top like I did!

—*"Weird Al" Yankovic*

MUSIC OVER TECHNOLOGY

Ultimately, great songs and great musicians are the most important recording tools. I believe you can record a great performance through a tin cup with a piece of string, and it'll still move you.

—*Ed Cherney*

Ed Cherney

SENSITIVITY

Toscanini did not make the orchestra nervous. If someone had a difficult solo, he would look the other way and concentrate on the other musicians.

—*Carmine Coppola*

WHAT IT TAKES

It all comes down to persistence and integrity.

—*Mark Isham*

BUILDING THE BAND

I picked the greatest musicians that I could find, who not only had chops and familiarity with a lot of different styles, but who also just loved playing. Having them in place, I can be pretty loose.
—*Paul Shaffer*

GIVING IT AWAY

We promoted our business by giving artists some free studio time in order to get credit on their albums or their films. This really motivated our growth. Potential clients would go to a big record store to find out that many of the top albums were recorded at Record Plant. And so that's where they wanted to record, too.
—*Chris Stone*

Chris Stone

GIVING IT UP

The hardest part of being an engineer/producer is to be willing to give of yourself to the project. To commit totally to what you are doing. And there *are* things you have to give up, like free time. But you get out of it what you put into it.
—*Bruce Swedien*

REINVENT, REDEFINE

Reinvent yourself constantly. As soon as you think you are cool and you know how to do something, the inspiration fades away. You have to continually redefine yourself, refine the operation, train your team, and stay active by taking on new and challenging projects.

—*Stevie Coss*

Stevie Coss

KNOW YOUR TARGET

You can't please everybody, so you have to aim at a particular market. Be specific in the direction you want to go.

—*Brian Holland*

U2 CAN DO IT

The band is very sincere, very heartfelt, very real. Every sound and part is questioned for its character and purpose. They are very focused on every single element that goes into the record. The thing that I learned from them was that there is not only one way to do something. There are fifty ways, and if you have the time, you will find them. And when you think you've got something great, it's amazing how you can find something even better.

—*David Tickle*

MOTIVATE

I try to be a motivating drummer. I help people around me play better because I push. I learned that from Bruce. He makes people play better.

—*Max Weinberg*

BE VALUABLE

Do what you love. Love what you do. Make people need your efforts and enthusiasm.

—*John Neff*

ONE DAY AT A TIME

Success is a moving target. I wake up and say, how can today be successful? How can I make today as valuable as yesterday? How can I contribute and be of value?

—*Patrick Monahan*

Patrick Monahan

BE GRATEFUL

Work harder than you ever imagined, always do your best at everything you take on, don't let anyone tell you it can't be done, and be very grateful that you get to listen to music all day for a living.

—*Sally Browder*

FINISH THE RACE

There are no losers, only winners who gave up too soon.

—*Hal Blaine*

FINDING YOUR IDENTITY

SENSE OF SELF

Being a musician gives me a sense of myself. I need that to have a real identity.

—*Michael McDonald*

ONE OF A KIND

I really like people who have a sound of their own, and a clear idea of how they sing and what they want to sing. And I really enjoy helping them to get it the way they want it.

—*Peter Asher*

FINDING YOUR PLACE

While you are acquiring the skill set, figure out what music you really love—music you really have an affinity for, the music that is natural to you. When you do that, you have found your place in music.

—*Glen Ballard*

SEEKING EUREKA

I'm an experimenter, an inventor. I'm always out there at the fringe, looking for new, unpredictable things to make and do.

—*Robert Moog*

Bob Moog

STAY REAL

Those who make it big usually make it big for about two years. If you do something that you don't believe in to make it real big, and then the big thing gets little, you're stuck with what you didn't believe in.
—*Mose Allison*

FOCUSED GROUP

I just sing and play and work with guys who really know how to put the sound down right. I don't really want to know much about what they do, because the more I get into it, the more confused I get.
—*Willie Nelson*

GROWING CONFIDENCE

I had a feeling that I was going to be some sort of superstar when I was a kid of ten or eleven. I used to get under the covers and say, "And now presenting *me* doing the great Al Jolson—'Mammmmmy'" . . . or "And now presenting me spelling Czechoslovakia!"
—*Harry Nilsson*

NO PAIN, NO FAME

Never had a spinal tap myself, but "memorable and painful" seemed to sum up what we wanted to be as a band.
—*Derek Smalls*

Derek Smalls

TV BLUES

The TV show that my sister, Moon, and I did bore no resemblance to the concept that was the original idea for the show. We were put through the TV wringer. Frank told us, "You really don't want to be involved in this industry. I know that you guys want to be excellent at what you do, and you're not allowed to be excellent at anything on TV."
—*Dweezil Zappa*

LASTING IMPRESSION

I persist because it's all I know how to do.
—*Frank Zappa*

MISTAKEN IDENTITY

Frank Zappa

We starved through '77 and '78. We were universally reviled as being too clever, and played too many chords to be real punks. We had all the volume, and the noise, and the speed of all the punk groups, but there was something wrong with us. We weren't genuine eighteen-year-olds who didn't know any better. We knew better, but we were playing for the energy of that scene.
—*Stewart Copeland*

IMAGE MATTERS

We needed an image, so we went down to see some friends of ours, the New York Dolls. We came back to the loft, put on makeup, lipstick, and rouge, and had our photo taken. It was ridiculous—we looked like four raging queens, and Gene looked like the biggest bull dyke we'd ever seen. We realized that this was not our look. A week later, Alice Cooper was playing Madison Square Garden, and

Peter Criss

we all went down for the show. We were in awe, and went back to the loft. We thought, what if there were *four* Alice Coopers?
—*Peter Criss*

GOTTA HAVE HEART

I go for artists that have definite character—a voice, a message, a simplicity—so you can hear the heart. It doesn't matter what the style or format is.
—*David Kershenbaum*

FAME OR SOMETHING LIKE IT

I run into people who say, "Jeeze, everybody knows who you are now," and others say, "God, where have you been, all these years?" I think they both might be right.
—*Leo Kottke*

PRE-MATURE

I was well-known when I was twenty-seven, but everybody thought I was sixty.
—*Taj Mahal*

EVERYONE KNOWS THIS IS NOWHERE

I don't live anywhere. On my income tax statement, I am listed as "Permanent Transient." When I have to be someplace, I go there, get a hotel, and set up shop, and then move on. I keep all my stuff in a warehouse. It's been like this for quite a while, which is kind of a weird way to live, but it works for me.

—*Pat Metheny*

VENERATE

Obviously, you have to draw from your influences, but there is a fine line between that and sheer copying. You have to believe in what you are doing, and have your own sound and approach to music. Draw from influences, but don't imitate.

—*Eddy Offord*

Eddy Offord

THE RIGHT SOUND AT THE RIGHT TIME

CSN's first record was brought out in a time of pre-heavy metal and stacks of Marshalls. We came out with this acoustic-feeling album, and it threaded right through everything and made its mark. We knew when we left the studio with that 2-track master that we had a hit record.

—*Graham Nash*

THE BLAINE IDENTITY

Almost everyone I had ever known tightened his drum heads as tight as he could. It's like talking in a high voice all the time, which was unnatural to me. Every instrument has a range, and the best quality is in the mid-range. I tuned to a mid-range and got a very fat tom-tom sound—boom, boom, boom, instead of ticka, ticka, ticka. It created a new sound on records that was identified with the West Coast.

—*Hal Blaine*

Hal Blaine

THE TRILL IS ON

I invented the "trill" that a lot of people use. I've always been crazy about the sound of bottleneck guitar and Hawaiian steel, and when I trill my hand, it kinda fools my ears a bit to make it sound like that. It became a habit, and I can hardly play a note now without shaking my hand.

—*B.B. King*

GOTTA PLEASE YOURSELF

I'm too good to be considered bad enough to be art, and I'm too bad to be considered good enough to be on country radio all the time. So, I do it for me, and if I satisfy me, that's the critical element. You have to start with what is honestly pleasing to yourself.

—*Dwight Yoakam*

THE GUY WITH THE BEARD

I'm probably known for my beard more than my playing. Not intentionally, I have created a persona that carries me along without business cards. I'm "that guy with the big beard."

—*Leland Sklar*

THE M.O. OF WAS (NOT WAS)

If Coltrane represents a prayer offered to the universe, Was (Not Was) is like itching powder, or the joke gum that turns your teeth black.
—*Don Was*

Don Was

JUST A ROCKER

I don't think of myself as being in the music industry. I think of myself as a die-hard rocker—somebody that just loves the whole idea of the backbeat. Turn up the amps, and let's knock the shit out of it.
—*Danny Kortchmar*

THE NAME GAME

THE VALUE OF A GOOD NAME

When I was growing up, T-Bone was one of those interesting names, like Ironjaw, or "Hard Rock" Lil. Howlin' Wolf used to have a piano player named Destruction. Just the name would conjure up enough for me to want to go and see them.

—*Taj Mahal*

STEELY DUDES

I can't think of any marital appliance I'd rather be identified with.

—*Walter Becker*

SYNTHESIS

We started using the word "synthesizer" three years after we began in 1967. We picked the word because synthesis means to create something from component parts. That's how you think of sound when you use a modular synthesizer.

—*Robert Moog*

Walter Becker

TOUGH GUYS

I had the experience of being in a shoe store when I was four years old, and this big kid came over and was threatening me. He said, "What's your name?" I told him "Dweezil," and he said it was a stupid name. I said, "What's your name?" He said "Buns." From that point, I never questioned the validity of my name.

—*Dweezil Zappa*

ED "BIG JULIE" CHERNEY

When you work with Quincy, you always get a nickname. Mine is "Svensk." Ed Cherney got his nickname from a delicatessen across from Westlake Studios on Wilshire Blvd., called "Big Julie's." We were always sending Ed over to get food, and after a while he just became known as Big Julie.

—*Bruce Swedien*

Bruce Swedien

THE CHIPMUNKS REVEALED

Theodore was Ted Keep, the mixer at 20th Century Fox; Simon was Sy Waronker, Lenny Waronker's father who started Liberty Records; and Alvin was Al Bennett, the president of Liberty Records.

—*Bruce Botnick*

CLEARLY BOB

The guitar player in the last band I was in found out what my name meant and started calling me Clearmountain. I got used to it, and when I started working in studios, everybody knew me by that name. Instead of "Hey, Bob," it was "Hey, Clearmountain."

—*Bob (Chiaramonte) Clearmountain*

POLICE YOURSELF

It just happened in the heady days of the punk boom, in the beginning, when suddenly there were groups with names that were hostile—the opposite of what we were familiar with. I just remember looking at a police car one day and thinking, well, there's some free promotion.

—*Stewart Copeland*

Stewart Copeland

BUT DON'T CALL ME RAY

It was a nickname in school, because I used to record onto cassettes when I was fifteen and sixteen. People used to call me "Dolby." When I started looking at the possibility of appearing professionally, it just made perfect sense.

—*Thomas "Dolby" Robertson*

SATELLITES AND MOTHER SHIPS

Today, virtually every artist can have his own studio. We call these smaller studios the "satellites," and the large, full service, 24/7 studios are the "mother ships."

—*Chris Stone*

BURNING SENSATIONS

There's a sexual maneuver called a "spinal tap," and I procured one of those in Singapore. It burned.

—*David St. Hubbins*

David St. Hubbins

LOOKING BACK

THAT TJB SOUND

The Tijuana Brass sound essentially was me playing all the trumpet parts. I was looking for my own identity as a musician, and the concept in the late fifties for the pop singers of the day was harmonizing with themselves or singing in unison. I was thinking of the Les Paul sound, with his guitar overdubs. I tried doing that in my little studio at home and came across some real interesting sounds for the trumpet.
—Herb Alpert

THE ONLY MIX

When we recorded "Tomorrow Never Knows," Paul had a tape recorder, and he found that by removing the erase head and putting a loop of tape on, he could saturate the tape with eternal sound by putting it into record. John, Ringo, and George went out and did the same and brought me these strange-sounding loops. We assembled them on machines all over the studio, and then had them continually going. It was like a primitive synthesizer—if you opened up a fader, you would hear it. That's when the mix became a performance. "Tomorrow Never Knows" can never be remixed again, because all those things happened at *that* time, in just *that* particular way.
—George Martin

WHY I STAND

Chicago and the Beach Boys were doing a stadium tour in the mid seventies. I was shooting basketball backstage in Washington, D.C., and I broke my leg after the gig. I had to stay the night in the hospital, and the band flew on and played the next show without me. But I made the next show after that, with a cast up to my ass. That was the first time I played keyboards standing up, and I have done it ever since.

—*Robert Lamm*

Robert Lamm

WHAT'S THAT SOUND?

It would be a groove to hear what Moses heard when he was up there on Mount Sinai.

—*Robert Moog*

MINIMALISM

I try not to confuse the ear with too many types of reverb. I often find one reverb setting that I am happy with and use it for everything. That certainly worked on *Dark Side of the Moon*. We only had one reverb going, as I remember.

—*Alan Parsons*

MOMMA MIA!

I remember when I went down to New York with the intention of establishing myself in the music business. I was in my early thirties, and my mother said to me, "Leonard, be careful—those people aren't like us." You know, she was right. They aren't like us.

—*Leonard Cohen*

Leonard Cohen

BUILDING THE WILBURYS

At night, after we'd finish the sessions on George Harrison's album, we'd have a drink and say, "Wouldn't it be great to have a group with anybody we want?" That's how it really came about. George said, "I'll have Bob Dylan," and I said, "Then I'll have Roy Orbison." We'd both known Tom Petty, and I had been working with him, and Tom seemed the ideal person, and it all fitted together.

—*Jeff Lynne*

THE LES PAUL GUITAR

It took years to get it really going. Mr. Berlin, who was the head of Gibson, and I were having dinner shortly before his death, and he asked me, "When you came to me with that broomstick with the pickup in 1941, did you ever believe in your wildest dreams that it was actually hockable?" Of course, I did. I was the only one who believed it at the time, but I never got discouraged.

—*Les Paul*

HAND CRAFTED EFFECTS

When we first put a voice and a guitar through those Leslie speakers, it was the most amazing sound ever. It was so tuneful and melodic. All the plug-in boxes now are derived from what had to be done mechanically, or by stretching tapes, or chopping tapes up, slowing tapes down.
—*Geoff Emerick*

Geoff Emerick

WRAPPING IT UP

It's chaotic at the end of a project. So many things begin to slip away that I've heard during the process, that there are moments when I think, is *this* the record I've been making all along?
—*Jackson Browne*

POLISHING STEELY DAN

I don't know of another band who were as meticulous in their recording. I remember an instance where they spent about three days on two bars of music.
—*Geordie Hormel*

Geordie Hormel

RECORD TIME

When I was recording with the Hollies, we cut our first album in an hour and a half—the entire record. We set up our instruments, and then we did our two 45-minute sets straight through. We knew what we were doing, because we'd been doing it for a couple of years. We took the best of both sets, and that was the first album.
—*Graham Nash*

SOUND FOR THE KING

Elvis asked if I could help with the live sound for his shows at the International, which later became the Hilton. I told him I had never done live sound in my life. He said I *had* to know more than the guys who were working at the time, because he couldn't even hear himself singing. So I took it over, set up some new stage monitors, redesigned the hotel's sound console, and worked with him there, and on the road, 'til the end. I was changing planes in Boston for our next show when I learned of his death.

—*Bill Porter*

MORRISON REMEMBERED

As much as he loved Paris and Paris loved him, Jim was a word man, and he couldn't communicate there. I think that alienation destroyed him psychologically.

—*Ray Manzarek*

Ray Manzarek

A REAL PIECE OF WORK

I still feel unemployed. It's like I don't really have a job. It's all so much fun, it's like a hobby, but luckily, I'm making a living at it.

—*"Weird Al" Yankovic*

THE ZAPPA TOUCH

He was essentially mixing from the stage, creating guitar tones that were unique but would cut through the arrangement that he created. He knew the range of the instruments in the accompaniment and the tones that they were creating, and he balanced his guitar tone to smoothly sit above everything. That's why his live recordings always sounded so good.

—*Dweezil Zappa*

IN THE SIXTIES

There were two terms revered in the days of cutting hits in the sixties. One was "dumb"—or expressing an emotion in a simple and honest way, as a teenager would. "Street" was the other word, meaning that someone like Darlene Love sings with conviction and puts across the simple, urban soulfulness of the New York street.

—*Paul Shaffer*

OOPS

The biggest mistakes I've made in my career were when I turned down big gigs that were offered to me—like when they asked me to play at Woodstock, and I turned it down to play another festival.

—*Dr. John*

Dr. John

DON'T BELIEVE YOUR HYPE

My big mistake was that I started believing all the hype. I believed that you *could* rock 'n' roll all night and party all day. I hit the very bottom in 1982, and going to rehab wasn't fashionable then.

—*Peter Criss*

FOND MEMORIES

GOOD CHEMISTRY

I'll never forget him walking down La Cienega Blvd. in all his Dr. John regalia, with his cane and his mojo, and the patchouli oil wafting down the street—and me in my beret. When we met, it was an incredible moment. I put my arm in his, and we became friends immediately. We strolled down the street. It was like a little movie.

—*Rickie Lee Jones*

Rickie Lee Jones

IT COMES AROUND

The first music I remember hearing was the Broadway cast album of *The Pajama Game*, which my mother played incessantly. It was John Raitt singing "Hey, There, You with the Stars in Your Eyes," that first got me. When I first met Bonnie, before producing her *Nick of Time* album, she had me call her dad's answering machine, where he sings that line and then says, "Hi, we're not home now..." It really came full circle when my mother called to hear it.

—*Don Was*

NICE START!

Paul had written "World Without Love," but the Beatles didn't want to do it. I had heard him sing it in passing because we were friends. I liked it a lot, but it was unfinished—didn't have a bridge. When we were picking songs for the first Peter and Gordon session, I said to Paul if he could finish it, we'd like to do it. He wrote the bridge, and it was one of the three or four songs we cut on our first recording session. That was our first single, and it went to number 1 all over the world. We got off to a very rapid and fortunate start.

—*Peter Asher*

ALWAYS ROOM FOR MORE

I did Van Dyke Parks' first album, *Song Cycle*. There was not one inch of blank space on any tune, and when we did find a section of blank space, he would find somebody, and we would put them on. He went out to dinner one night to a Hungarian restaurant and came back with half a dozen Hungarian violin players. He composed something on the spot, and we added them to one of the songs.

—*Lee Herschberg*

Lee Herschberg

AUDITIONING CHRISTINA AGUILERA

She stood there, sixteen years old, her eyes went into sort of an icy stare—a total sense of self-possession and perfect intonation. She had the complete command of a seasoned performer in Carnegie Hall. No inhibition, no sense of containment. In that moment, you knew you were in the room with greatness. If it happens one or two more times in my life, I'll consider myself very lucky.

—*Ron Fair*

OUTLAW NERVE

When I started out to be a songwriter, I admired the people who were good at it, and Johnny Cash and Willie Nelson were right up there at the top. Then to be up there on stage with them singing along on these songs I grew up with—it was such a wonderful thing, but I'm sure it drove 'em crazy sometimes. One time, John said to me, "I don't think there's another person in the world who would have the nerve to sing harmony with me on 'Folsom Prison.'"
—*Kris Kristofferson*

CHAIRMAN OF THE BOARD

Frank Sinatra was my idol. As a kid, I used to play hooky from school and take the subway over from Brooklyn to see him at the Paramount Theatre in New York. Recording with him was one of the biggest thrills of my career.
—*Al Schmitt*

Al Schmitt

"A DAY IN THE LIFE"

The gradual long fade, done manually, was monumental. To make that end crescendo loud—the orchestra was told to go from A to E in thirty-seven bars. I was pulling up the faders as the song progressed because I knew that I needed another 6 dB by the time I got to the end.
—*Geoff Emerick*

RUBBER SOULS

It was such a thrill to work on John's unfinished tracks with Paul, George and Ringo, because it sounded just like the Beatles, which it was, of course. A lot of things were magical simply because when Paul plays piano and bass, it sounds like him. When George plays guitar, it sounds like him. When they sing harmonies, it sounds like them.
—*Jeff Lynne*

LUCKY STARS

I think I'm probably the luckiest person in the world, to be able to work with people like Sting, who are making albums for the sake of music, not just for making a hit record.

—*Hugh Padgham*

DUTCH TREAT

When we performed in Amsterdam in 1974, the Rolling Stones came to see us. I couldn't believe those guys would do that for us—*that* was a feeling of having arrived.

—*Bill Payne*

Bill Payne

SPECTOR IN MY LIVING ROOM

Phil used to rehearse in my living room. I'd come home from Junior High, and there was Phil, Marshall, and Annette rehearsing "To Know Him Is to Love Him"—1958. When I went away to camp that summer, they put the record out, and all of a sudden Phil was on American Bandstand with a number 1 record.

—*Russ Titelman*

EARLY TIMES WITH DAVE

I spent months on end with Dave Matthews at his house in Virginia, helping with the preproduction. We'd sit around with a couple of guitars, and he'd be pouring out all these little musical ideas that would eventually become some of his biggest hits, like "Crash into Me," "Too Much," "Crush," "Stay," and so on. I feel mighty lucky to know him and to have worked with him.

—*John Alagia*

COSTUME PARTY

I'd seen pictures of Zappa and thought he was the scariest person I'd ever seen. When I got the call to play on *Lumpy Gravy*, I decided to go in with pajama bottoms and weird clothes—before it was hip to wear pajama bottoms. I walked in and Frank came over, introduced himself and said, "I like your costume." I told him I liked his, too.

—*Tommy Tedesco*

Tommy Tedesco

STRIKING GOLD

We always knew when things were going well in the studio because the producer, Jerry Wexler, would get up and dance around like John Huston in *The Treasure of the Sierra Madre*—the scene where the old prospector discovers gold.

—*Carlos Santana*

TWEENER BLUES

My father was a doctor, and T-Bone Walker was one of his patients. He used to come over and play at our parties. I learned to play lead guitar from T-Bone at my house when I was eleven.

—*Steve Miller*

4

TECHNOLOGY

INVENTING

BRINGING THINGS TOGETHER

I didn't really design the parametric equalizer; I built it. It was an idea that was waiting to happen—a circuit that was waiting for the right kind of op-amp and the right application.
—*George Massenburg*

George Massenburg

THE RIPPLE EFFECT

In retrospect, it seems that most of what I've done have been mistakes of one sort or another. And every mistake that I've made has rippled through my life, influencing other things that I've done.
—*Robert Moog*

SYNCHRONICITY

No matter what I'm thinking of, there's no reason for me to think that there aren't many others thinking the same thing. It's odd, but you can think of something and actually build it or patent it and then find out that it's already been sitting out there somewhere.
—*Les Paul*

WILD CARDS

We must have people who have an impeccable, flawless knowledge of the technology, but there will be no progress unless there are also people with strange ideas.

—*Roger Lagadec*

PERSEVERANCE

Solutions don't appear miraculously. They are the result of a lot of hard work, a lot of burning the midnight oil, and a lot of intense frustration from doing it the wrong way until you find the right way.

—*Rupert Neve*

Roger Lagadec

THE SCIENCE OF SOUND

ANYTHING GOES

I'm very much into playing things because of the quality of the sound and not just because of the notes. It doesn't have to be a musical sound. I've made some samples in my studio using a big spring, for example. I hit it, scraped it with metal, wood, my thumb, and snapped it. I used it to make a rhythm track, and for the bass drum, I sampled hitting a piece of cardboard. I hear a sound that interests me, and I find a way to use it.

—*Herbie Hancock*

Herbie Hancock

TECHNO-MUSIC. GET USED TO IT.

Music and technology are intertwined. Like a double helix, this DNA of music and technology cannot be separated. You ignore it at your peril as a musician.

—*Glen Ballard*

WE'VE GOT THE WHOLE WORLD IN OUR HANDS

I have always been interested in the notion that if you wanted to release what you have done to the entire world, you could just do it. Now we have the technology to do so.

—*Jon Brion*

MACHINE INTELLIGENCE

Inanimate objects, especially when they have working parts and depend on things like sound and light, are susceptible to the influence of the people who are working with them.

—*Leonard Cohen*

CAR TALK

Studio playback is not realistic when compared to the usual listening environment of the audience. The car has always been the place where you have your radio—where you really hear things for the first time.

—*David Foster*

HYBRID MUSIC

There are sound effects, and there are sounds that bridge the gap between sound effects and music.

—*David Lynch*

David Lynch

BIRTH OF THE MOOG

These were the building blocks. You had one module—one circuit that made a waveform, another circuit that filtered it, a third that shaped the loudness, and then you had a keyboard controller, and you could interconnect these things. The voltage from one controlled the other, and you built on that to make a complex sound.

—*Robert Moog*

THE ELECTRONIC MUSICIAN

I'm an "electronic kind of guy." An earlier era might have offered more in terms of aesthetics, but so much of what I do involves electronic devices that I don't think I would be happy without them.

—*Frank Zappa*

SPECIAL EQUIPMENT?

I use the Kaori X30, an experimental compressor that actually increases your guitar's atomic weight.

—*David St. Hubbins*

PRACTICE AT HOME

Sometimes when you go into a hired studio—an engineer, the band all waiting for you to tell them what to do—you really feel lost. But you can learn to deal with it by working at home with your own tools. Even if you don't know the exact compressor you want, or the microphone—don't be afraid. Your power and your gift aren't going to go away because the kick drum doesn't sound just as you imagined it in your mind.

Lisa Coleman

—*Lisa Coleman*

IT'S A MIRACLE

I think just the fact that music can come up a wire is a miracle.

—*Ed Cherney*

FEAR OF KNOBS

The producer with the Band in the early days, John Simon, took the mystery out of mixing consoles for me. He simplified it: "It's just a bunch of tone and volume controls." People go into studios, and they look at the board, and think it's really intimidating. What they don't realize is that it's a whole bunch of the same thing over and over again.
—*Robbie Robertson*

VINYL LIVES

I've always liked vinyl, but it doesn't sound like the original. Some of the things that people like about vinyl— like that softer, less harsh sound— occur when it's being pressed. If you want to retain the edge with vinyl, there is no way to do it without getting distortion.
—*Bernie Grundman*

Bernie Grundman

TAKE YOUR TIME

Since the advent of the sequencer, as a writer, you have been able to postpone a lot of decisions until later, about the structure of a song, about tempos, keys, about the choice of instrumentation.
—*Thomas Dolby*

CLEAR CHANNELS

When I produce or mix a record, I hear the music in a sort of sonic spectrum. If you have too many things in the same register, it's going to be harder to hear them. So, I work on making a big sound out of as few elements as possible.
—*Hugh Padgham*

SUBTLE MOVES

Tommy Dowd taught me about the subtleties of microphone placement. He was very meticulous. He'd move the mic an inch, and it would change the sound.

—*Al Schmitt*

THE HUMAN FACE OF TECHNOLOGY

What we need is technology with a human face—the human interface—so that the technology makes itself disappear.

—*Roger Lagadec*

THE NATURE OF MUSIC

Maybe I'm old-fashioned, but I think the sound of a natural instrument is the best. One of the dangers of all this technology, synthesized sound, and mechanics is that it can make the music a bit sterile.

—*George Martin*

George Martin

RECORDING

SOUND RESULTS

You have to be into every aspect of the recording process if you are going to get a good sound. You have to know all about what you are doing and what is related to it. Otherwise, you can't get the results that you want.

—*David Lindley*

David Lindley

A CLEAR PATH

What I listen for is transparency, where the idea moves from its inception to the listener with the least amount of forces impeding it.

—*George Massenburg*

BEST OF BOTH

In the early days when I worked with engineers, I warned them, "Be ready to record at the drop of a hat. All I am going for is feeling. If you can capture a good sound while it feels good—bonus. Don't fool around trying to get this perfect mic on the instrument if I have something really rolling in the studio." That was always the prerequisite— the feeling. As I progressed with that and hopefully got a little wiser, I realized that I could get both.

—*Herb Alpert*

RAPPORT

There are microphones that are more or less sensitive to the kinds of sounds that I can produce. Engineers know about those things. But there is also some other kind of process at work. Once you start to hear the playbacks, you can accommodate yourself to the microphone, and the microphone begins to accommodate itself to you.

—*Leonard Cohen*

TAKE A CHANCE

People ask us how we work, but in the course of a day it's usually fairly spontaneous. There's no specific route. We just try things, and the first thing that sounds good, we keep.

—*Mitchell Froom*

Mitchell Froom

JUST DO IT YOURSELF

With high quality recording gear way down in price, it's worth investing in some level of gear. You learn so much more when you play with the knobs and put a different musical perspective on the work.

—*Peter Gabriel*

DON'T MISS A BEAT

What we needed was a mic going all the time, getting sounds and reactions, so we could use them whenever we wanted. All of our best stuff was never on tape. We'd be working and really getting into something, and then we'd go to the studio and go, "1, 2, 3..." and it wouldn't be the same.

—*John Lennon*

GIVE IT A TRY

I don't know the terminology, and I didn't go to school as an engineer, but I engineer all my projects, and I like to experiment. I don't care if a particular microphone is only supposed to be used on guitar and hi-hats and snares. I'll try it as a room mic and then compress the hell out of it and put some distortion on it and then throw it back into the room through amps. I'll go through all these sounds until I find things that I like.

—*Linda Perry*

GOING FOR THE GOLD

There is a competitive side to making great music and finding ways for it to slot better, to sound better, to be heard in a different way than ever before. When you start a new record, there is no cushion under your ass.

—*Phil Ramone*

Phil Ramone

HOME SWEET STUDIO

The recording studio is just about the best place to be on an afternoon. You've got your couch, your air-conditioning, all those knobs, great speakers. There is no hi-fi after you've worked in a recording studio. It's never going to sound as good as it sounds when you are hearing a master.

—*Walter Becker*

STEELY WALL OF SOUND

I like to hear things come out from side to side. When I mixed *Aja*, I hard panned a lot of stuff, including reverbs. If I had a Fender Rhodes, I'd have it dry on one side, and the reverb return only on the other side. You'd hear it jump out a little.

—*Elliot Scheiner*

Elliot Scheiner

KICKING ME SOFTLY

I'm a pretty gentle person, and I think that puts people at ease and allows the artist to do the job better. At the same time, I am concerned with getting really beefy, kick-butt tracks.

—*Terry Becker*

FIDDLING WITH THE SOUND

Acoustic fiddles are a bitch because every fiddle and fiddle player is totally different. EQ is just awful for fiddles. The more you EQ a fiddle, the more it sounds wanky.

—*Ray Benson*

SPONTANEITY

I like a sense of abandon in the studio, and I try to work fast, not getting hung up on things that won't be remembered six months later. I don't usually think things out beforehand. I like to jam.

—*Tchad Blake*

DON'T LOSE A GOOD THING

When you've got a particular sound that is inspiring the musicians, don't be afraid to take that effect and print it to the track, along with the performance. If you're insecure about that, maybe print the effect to an additional track, so that every time you push up the mix, the mood that the effect created is always there.

—*Kevin Killen*

Kevin Killen

WHATEVER TURNS YOU ON

The most important things are the music, the songs, and the performances. If you use a mic that I wouldn't use for hammering nails and it works, then that's great. It doesn't matter. Whatever you are comfortable with using is what's right.

—*Bob Clearmountain*

EASY EXCESS

Every new recording technique that comes out usually starts very tastefully and then gets overdone.

—*Eddy Offord*

TAKE CARE

When I was a kid, my uncle had the first independent recording studio in New York City, and I used to go there on Saturdays and watch him record. He told me that you had to work with this equipment as if you were a watchmaker, and you were working on a very delicate watch. I was in awe of this and learned to take good care of the equipment.

—*Al Schmitt*

THE SECRET OF A GREAT MIX

Find out what the client wants, and give him a great sounding version of it. If the client doesn't love it, it doesn't matter how great it is.
—*Michael C. Ross*

Michael C. Ross

THE EDITING IRONY

The changeover to digital editing was so anti-intuitive. With razor blade editing, you focused on the parts you didn't want, and you took those out. With digital editing, you have to focus on the parts that you *do* want and put them together.
—*Harry Shearer*

CURB FUNCTION LUST

People are dismayed because certain mixes sound awful on DAWs. Most of the problem starts with the home enthusiast buying a system and paying a lot of money for plug-ins—and then using all of them, or as many as possible, to make something sound better. This "Function Lust" is not a very useful concept in the mixing of music.
—*George Massenburg*

LIVING ROOMS

When we started out, studios were like hospitals—fluorescent lights, white walls, and hardwood floors. My partner, Gary Kellgren, turned them into living rooms. The greatest compliment an artist could pay us was, "I'd like to live here!" And sure enough, they would.
—*Chris Stone*

TIPS AND TECHNIQUES

TALK IT THROUGH

There are ways to make things brighter or darker by asking the musicians to help you, instead of not saying anything, and messing around with the EQ. The danger is that you might alter the way they play. If they hear more bottom, they might start laying off those bottom strings.
—*Greg Ladanyi*

Greg Ladanyi

GET IT TOGETHER

When getting sounds, mixing or tracking, I listen to everything, or as much as I can, together. A common error is to get a great kick sound, then solo the snare, then the overheads, etc. It's best to have it all in, right from the start.
—*Tchad Blake*

GET THE WHOLE PICTURE

I think you can fool yourself into thinking that a track sounds great, because everything in rock 'n' roll is based on drums. If you take the drums away and it's still rocking, then you know you have something that is pretty reasonable.
—*Alan Parsons*

CHECK THE MONO MIX

Many folks aren't driving with two speakers on at the same time at the same level where you are sitting while you are engineering. Some of those wonderful effects you spend hours and hours creating don't translate. Constantly switching back and forth between mono and stereo helps you beat that problem.

—*Phil Ramone*

THE MOTOWN EDGE

We used a lot of compressors and limiters, so we could pack the songs full and make them jump out of the radio. We wanted to keep the levels hot on the records so that they were louder than anyone else's.

—*Brian Holland*

TIPS FROM STEELY DAN

If you never play the root of a chord, nobody will be able to tell if you make a mistake.

—*Roger Nichols*

Roger Nichols

INSIDE SOUND

I open up the piano lid and move my head around inside the piano until I find a good spot. I note where the center of my eyes are and put the center of the middle capsule there.

—*Nathaniel Kunkel*

HAVE GEAR, WILL TRAVEL

As an engineer gets more work, he acquires equipment that he needs for his projects. A lot of times, engineers rent it back to their clients. I've never done that because I felt there might be resentment in the end. My philosophy is that when they hire me as an engineer, they get what I have.

—Elliot Scheiner

THE SOUND CHANGED

We took the bottom skins off Ringo's tom-toms and put the mic up inside. Prior to that, you probably found one overhead mic, one bass mic, and one snare mic on the drums. This gave us the slap of the top with no resonance of the bottom skin. In my opinion, *Revolver* was the album to change all sounds. Better than *Pepper*, from a sound point of view.

—Geoff Emerick

WHAT THE DRUMMER HEARS

A lot of people forget to listen behind the drummer, as if you are in the playing position. It's good to stand in front of the drum kit, but if you don't go on the other side you are missing an entirely different picture.

—Robert Carranza

Robert Carranza

LEAVE SPACE

One of my main techniques is the illusion of space, especially around vocals and the rhythmic elements. It's really something that I do by ear—work on it until I have a sound that is personal, emotional, and isn't trying too hard.

—Kevin Killen

THE MIXING MIND

I try to discover the vision of the artist. Then I study the song and where the dynamics are in the recording. I'm trying to build on the things I don't need to change, let the tracks speak for themselves, and make adjustments as necessary.

—*Dave Reitzas*

MAGIC GLUE

I use analog tape for stereo mix down, mostly 1-inch, sometimes 1/2-inch. I find analog tape saturation and compression in the bottleneck stage of the mixing process to be some sort of "magic glue." It smoothes the top end and tightens the bottom.

—*Tal Herzberg*

Tal Herzberg

KEYBOARD LOGIC

I'm mortified when I see people recording a piano with a mic over the low strings and another over the high strings. That has nothing to do with how a piano sounds. To me, that is left-right mono and not very interesting. I usually use a coincident pair to preserve the overall image. The low frequencies are nondirectional anyway, so you will hear them on both mics. That's a fact, and there's nothing you can do about it.

—*Bruce Swedien*

THAT OL' 47

We had one old Neumann U-47 tube microphone that I used in Nashville into a console with Langevin preamps, which gave an unusual impedance-loading characteristic to the mic. This enhanced the "presence" quality and gave a special sound to Elvis, Roy Orbison, the Everly Brothers, and just about every vocalist we worked with. People always used to comment about the unique sound of the vocals.

—*Bill Porter*

PUT ON A HAPPY PHASE

If you're going to use ten mics on a drum kit and the mics are out of phase with each other, your drum sound will suck.

—*Eddie DeLena*

Eddie DeLena

FAUX FRETLESS

Over the years, I have converted all of my basses to mandolin frets. I love the way they feel, since I like to glissando, and it's so minimal. Put a little harmonizer on, and all of a sudden, it sounds like a fretless.

—*Leland Sklar*

LAURIE ANDERSON IN THE STUDIO

We had one song where the loop was a grouping of seventeen piano notes, counted over a bar of eleven beats. This was the rhythm track, and my job was to punch in as we recorded other instruments. We ended up giving each note a letter, A through Q, and we would sing the alphabet over and over as we worked. "OK, punch in at M"—it just couldn't be counted

Leanne Ungar

numerically. When the song was finished, it was mixed without the loop, and no one ever heard it but us. I still sing it when I hear the song, "Langue D'Amour."

—*Leanne Ungar*

BACKWARD GUITAR

Acoustic guitar has a lot of transient information, so when you turn it backwards, it sounds like a bowed instrument, with an eerie backwards quality. The result is a mysterious orchestral sound.
—*Dweezil Zappa*

PLANT EASTER EGGS

If you can make a record that is instantly appealing but afterwards you discover stuff—to me, that is the ultimate goal. That's what Beatles and Stevie Wonder records do. After decades of playing those records, it's still fun listening.
—*Jon Brion*

OLDIES BUT GOODIES

People are working with the latest digital tools and computerized consoles loaded with all the latest high-speed tricks—and what do they plug into this incredible state-of-the-art starship? They plug in a fifty-year-old microphone. I love it!
—*Stephen Paul*

Stephen Paul

5

TAKING CARE OF BUSINESS

THE GOOD, THE BAD, THE UGLY

THE BUSINESS OF MUSIC

I like it, but what can you say—it's like any other business. You've got the same problems, you've got politics to deal with. The competition is fierce.
—*Lindsey Buckingham*

THE COST OF DOING BUSINESS

At one point, we had eight semi-trailers, a Lear jet, three busses, and eighty-five guys working for us. Each show alone cost a million.
—*Peter Criss*

Lindsey Buckingham

DEMAND EXCEEDING SUPPLY

In those early days of punk, the phenomenon was bigger than the supply of music to fulfill the need. Because of the nature of these bands, many couldn't get it together to get their records out.
—*Stewart Copeland*

STAY ON TOP OF IT

My old accountant stole all my money. I made the mistake of giving him power of attorney, and the money just disappeared. My advice is to sign all your own checks and don't trust anybody.

—*Steve Lukather*

THE TIME IT TAKES

For *Mother's Milk*, we were thrust into a situation and had to make it or break it under the duress of being a reborn band with a new guitar player and a new drummer. Before *Blood Sugar Sex Magik*, we went on tour for two years, and after the road, we had the time to write and get down to business, work it out in a rehearsal studio, assemble songs that we were in love with. It was what we were all about, without rushing.

—*Anthony Kiedis*

Anthony Kiedis

BEING PREPARED

TAKE CARE OF BIZ

People try to convince musicians that if they go into the business area, it will take away from their music. It does *not* take away from their music—it makes it better, because it opens up their minds.
—*David Lindley*

GET GOOD ADVICE

Get a good lawyer, and listen to him. You always need your own person to fight for you. And sometimes, you need several, to keep them in balance with each other.
—*Suzanne Vega*

IT'S NOT JUST ABOUT THE MONEY

Fortunately, or unfortunately, the art and the music and the money go

Suzanne Vega

together, and you have to be precise about what that means to you. You need to be disciplined, and you cannot go in unprepared.
—*Phil Ramone*

SIMPLE TRUTH

Pay attention. Be prepared. Learn from your mistakes. Listen.
—*Dave Reitzas*

MIND YOUR TAXES

Figure out everything you can write off, and save receipts.
—*Silas Hite*

PLAY THE GAME

The key is to be aware it's show *business*. The ego is the "show" part, but the bigger word is "business." There will always be some guy in a flashy suit telling you what to do.
—*Mark Hudson*

Silas Hite

STARTING A BUSINESS

For anyone starting any kind of business, there is a formula, but many creative people don't really understand how a business works. You start out with a feasibility study to prove to yourself that your idea is a viable one. You then proceed to a business plan that is designed to prove to others that your concept is good, and it is a tool to raise money, to get investors, to find loans. Then you put together your team and find the people that don't do what you do, so that you can allow them to handle the various positions necessary. You want all the bases covered when you go into business.
—*Chris Stone*

IT'S THE LAW

Get the best attorney you can afford.
—*Eddie Kramer*

Eddie Kramer

TIPS FROM THE TOP

BE COOL

I think you can be tough without screaming and yelling. When I know I am right and I know what I want, I can be fairly firm. I'm sure there are occasions where someone who is prepared to jump up and down and yell could elicit a few more cents out of the deal than perhaps I could. On the other hand, I prefer things to remain on a congenial basis whenever possible.

—*Peter Asher*

Peter Asher

RESPECT YOUR AUDIENCE

The public can discern the difference between a cynical marketing plan and something heartfelt. Have a good thing, and do it honestly and sincerely.

—*Will Ackerman*

PRETZEL LOGIC

Our motto has been, "Lose money on every deal; make it up in volume."

—*Walter Becker*

WHO'S THE BOSS?

Make sure the boss is real happy with your work, and he won't fire you. And if you don't know who the boss is, take a look out from the stage. That's the boss.

—*Chris Isaak*

SELL GRACEFULLY

Don't oversell the deal. If you've made your point, don't push it. When you win your argument, don't run the guy into the ground.

—*Harry Nilsson*

Harry Nilsson

RETURN YOUR CALLS

Even if it's uncomfortable, or you have to say no to someone, it's good to communicate that. And you can do it with dignity, in a way that leaves that person with self-respect. You tell the truth and create goodwill and harmony.

—*David Kershenbaum*

IF YOU BUILD IT, WILL THEY COME?

Find out what your target demographic is. Who are the people who are going to use your service? What is unique about your service, in terms of what you are offering against your competition? And last: your marketing. If you build it, that is not enough if the customers don't know you are there. The marketing, promotion, publicity, and the Web sites are all very important.

—*Chris Stone*

SAVE A FRIEND

The only way you can stay friends in business is to keep business business and friends friends. Verbal deals just don't work. If you want to save that friendship, go to a lawyer, and put it in writing.

—*Shelly Yakus*

PRICING THEORY
Always charge slightly less than your client will expect.
—*Martin Böhm*

TRY THIS AT HOME
The main business trick is seduction—and letting the other person think they are winning.
—*Andy Summers*

Martin Böhm

ANOTHER BUSINESS TRICK
Wad up a little piece of flash paper, and put it in an ashtray when no one is looking. Later, when you're at a key point of discussion, light a cigarette, and drop the match into the ashtray, and you get a big flash that instantly disappears. It knocks your opponent off guard.
—*Steve Miller*

DON'T FORGET
Ignore all advice.
—*Derek Smalls*

Derek Smalls

KEEPING IT REAL

RULE #1
Don't cheat people.
—*Al Kooper*

RULE #2
Diversify or die.
—*Chris Stone*

Al Kooper

TAKE CARE OF BUSINESS
If you don't have the business side together, the money won't follow. There are too many good musicians who screw up business-wise, and then people don't want to hire them anymore. It's very important to surround yourself with people who reflect your work and your integrity. You gotta be straight, and you gotta know your job.
—*George Duke*

THE COMPANY YOU KEEP
The record company is not basically your enemy. They are there to work with you and to help promote your career. Don't regard them as an enemy, until they are.
—*Rickie Lee Jones*

THE BOTTOM LINE

People think this is such a glamorous business. They jump in with both feet, rarely looking back until it's too late. One of the reasons I have been able to buy out so many studios is because many people approach building a studio without ever seriously considering the profitability aspect.

—Allen Sides

Allen Sides

COMMON SENSE

Most business is common sense. You figure out what things mean and what you want to accomplish. If you are not afraid to ask when you don't know, and apply common sense when you do—it works.

—Peter Asher

PRIORITIES

Keep your eye on the donut and not on the hole.

—David Lynch

DOING BUSINESS IN THE MUSIC BUSINESS

Business is very, very easy. Give everybody their fair share and don't drive yourself crazy over nickel-and-dime stuff in your contracts. The Doors did a four-way split. Morrison, God bless him, said, "We all do something, but then we put it into the Doors' mind, and out come Doors' songs. Let's just make it a four-way split." And it's been easy ever since.

—Ray Manzarek

GET IT IN WRITING

I am very trustful of people, but it's important to be clear. It's perfectly okay to say, "Before we go to work on Monday, we need a proper piece of paper."

—*Phil Ramone*

TRICKY BUSINESS

There are basic rules in how to straddle that area between commerce and art, but I think that you should never let the business part get in the way of what you're really about musically. It can trick you into doing things that you are not really meant to do. You might even be successful at doing them, but I think that the bottom line is not to betray your gift and make it a cheap thing.

—*Robbie Robertson*

Robbie Robertson

THE THING WITH GROWTH

It's a reality of business that once things get to a certain size, a corporate aspect creeps in. And I think it's probably essential.

—*Will Ackerman*

MUTUAL FIDELITY

Bruce Springsteen taught me how to work hard. If he hadn't been the *mensch* he is, he might have said that the drummer was not making it and brought somebody else in. He gave me the room to develop. When you think about the lack of loyalty in the music business, this was an incredible thing to do.

—*Max Weinberg*

FOLLOW THROUGH

When I sign an artist, I make their music my cause and become an advocate for them—much more than just delivering a great record and a great song. It's seeing it through the promotion and marketing, publicity, and distribution levels of bringing it to fruition.

—*Ron Fair*

BUSINESS IS BUSINESS

There is only one rule: If you sell records, you can make more records. If you don't sell records, you don't make any more records. It makes breathtaking sense.

—*Laurie Anderson*

ACTION ITEM

Don't stay in the middle of nowhere and expect to be discovered. Sitting around being a tortured artist is not going to get you anywhere. You have to go knock on doors, show people what you can do, and go where the action is.

—*Andy Paley*

Andy Paley

THE MONEY PART

WHERE'S THE MONEY?

You can still make money in this business, but it's a defining moment for those who are into music because they love it, and for those who just want to make money.

—*Glen Ballard*

Glen Ballard

IT'S NOT ABOUT THE MONEY

It's singing the songs and working in clubs that has kept me alive. I never made any money on my records. The only money I made from records was from the mechanical licenses when Van Morrison, or the Who, or other artists recorded my songs. According to the record companies, my records have never made money.

—*Mose Allison*

MUSIC AND $$$

Many musicians love playing so much that they would do it for free, and there is always somebody out there who will allow them to.

—*Paul Shaffer*

INVEST WISELY

If you are going to make the kind of money where you warrant having a serious business manager/accountant, find someone good who will invest the money for you. Find someone who is conservative and pays your taxes—wisely.

—*Lindsey Buckingham*

SAFE KEEPING

Because we were at 8th Avenue and 44th Street, which is kind of a rough neighborhood, my wife would get the payroll cash from the bank and put it in our son's diaper for safekeeping and then bring it down to the studio. Sometimes people got wet money.

—*Chris Stone*

Chris Stone

SURVIVAL

Don't sell your publishing, because that's how you'll live when things aren't going well.

—*Rickie Lee Jones*

NEVER ENOUGH

Everybody, no matter what their financial status, is nervous to a certain extent about maintaining whatever style their income led to. If I were ten times richer, I would probably still feel just as neurotic about paying my rent.

—*Stewart Copeland*

GET A PLAN

I've spent my life working my ass off in the studio, and like many of us who concentrate on the music, we're ripe to be ripped off. Get a good retirement plan.

—*Mike Shipley*

THE $ECRET

To be successful in business, it's always a good idea to make lots and lots and lots of money.
—*"Weird Al" Yankovic*

"Weird Al" Yankovic

6

THE
LIFESTYLE

TOO MUCH OF A GOOD THING

LIVING ON THE EDGE

A rock 'n' roll musician lives on the edge of good and bad, positive and negative. You walk the gauntlet of total pleasure, happiness, completion—and excess, drug addiction or crashing in cars, like James Dean, one of the first rock 'n' rollers.
—*Paul Kantner*

THE COST OF FAME

I've never wanted big-time success because, to me, it suggested the dangers and excesses of fame.
—*Van Dyke Parks*

Van Dyke Parks

THE INDUSTRY MACHINE

I saw the machine greased up to the max in Fleetwood Mac during the *Rumours* time, and I was a bit ambivalent about all that. There was a focus on the phenomenon and the soap opera aspect. It became a little more important than the music, in a way. There was also the momentum of that machine, and the idea that "If it works, then run it into the ground."
—*Lindsey Buckingham*

THE IMAGE

People are attracted to the celebrity image, and it's easy to get lost if you become successful. And there are a lot of successful people who got lost.
—*Rickie Lee Jones*

$ANITY

I quit the business every time I started to make any money. I've been told that if I had stayed in it, I'd have been worth an awful lot. Either you save your money and lead a normal life, or you take the chance to live like an emperor. I thought, let's see what that's about—and I did. I gave orders and people jumped. One day I looked in the mirror and said to myself, "You're nuts." So, I quit. I realized I was losing what sanity I was born with.
—*Artie Shaw*

Artie Shaw

KISS GOODBYE

I was getting tired with the band because we were becoming dolls, lunchboxes, and pinball machines. As a musician, I was frustrated. And the makeup! At first it was great, but after a while, I couldn't stand it.
—*Peter Criss*

MISFITS AND RUDE BEHAVIOR

ROCK 'N' ROLL REBEL

I was a crank as a child, a real malcontent. I was into *Mad Magazine*, and anything that said the adult world was a joke. Then John Lennon came along, and he wore that attitude on his sleeve.

—*Marshall Crenshaw*

Marshall Crenshaw

DO THE MASHED POTATO

We had sessions with a female singer who used to strip and wanted to be hit with hot mashed potatoes right before recording.

—*Martin Böhm*

SHOWER THE PEOPLE YOU LOVE

I idolized Frank Zappa, Captain Beefheart, and loved sixties underground music. My band, the Deadbeats, played jazz-punk—really rude, loud, and rowdy, with power chords off flat-5s in a primitive rhythmic setting. At one gig at the Whisky, I threw seaweed at the audience. We were either loved or hated by the punk audiences.

—*Geza X*

THE PARANOIDS ARE AFTER ME

I used to get letters after I won the Rhodes scholarship—wackos saying that Rhodes scholars are the problem with this country; they get trained as spies. Years later, a guy at the airport asked me, "Is it true, Mr. Kristofferson, that you are a Soviet intelligence agent educated at Oxford?" I said, "Take a good look in my eyes and say 'intelligence' again."

—*Kris Kristofferson*

GIMMICKS GONE BAD

It seemed so perfect to get out there and have no worries or cares—the intense, zany freedom of life. But journalists are always looking to pigeon-hole musicians into a little fashion quadrant, taking away from the depth and giving it a superficial label. What we are really doing is expressing the deepest love and musical compassion that we can muster up.

—*Anthony Kiedis*

Anthony Kiedis

THEY GOT DOWN

Those who wrote most of the classical music, at least in the eighteenth century, did not tend to be stuffy people. Mozart was a party animal. And Beethoven got mad at a waiter once and dumped a bowl of spaghetti on his head.

—*Peter Schickele*

ROOM SERVICE

We did it all, threw TVs out of the hotel windows. We bought power tools and knocked holes in the walls to connect our rooms in one hotel. It was like a challenge to see how far we could go.

—*Peter Criss*

FLYING ON THE JEFFERSON AIRPLANE

I got spiked when we were doing the first Hot Tuna album. I thought I was drinking apple juice. I was working in a remote truck, and I was ready to go, and all of a sudden the sides of the truck started to breathe.

—*Al Schmitt*

NOT THAT PARTY!

Everyone eventually gets burnt out in the sessions, and we used to do a thing where when someone would fall asleep on the couch in the control room, they would get covered with bits of scotch tape and cigarette butts and wake up covered up with all this garbage, and then we would photograph them. It became a horrendous running gag. We called it "taking people to the party."

—*Andy Summers*

Andy Summers

HANDLING REJECTION

SHOCKING BEHAVIOR

I believe the booing at the Newport Folk Festival was misinterpreted. The reason people booed us was because Bob Dylan was the star of the event, and many people waited three days to see him, and he only played fifteen minutes—just three songs. We had never performed together live and only rehearsed once the night before. It was sloppy and not what people were expecting. And no one prepared them for the fact that he would be electrified.

—*Al Kooper*

LATER THAT YEAR...

When we played Forest Hills later that summer, they had read in the papers that they were supposed to boo us. "Like a Rolling Stone" was number 1 by that time, so they booed us, and then they sang along.

—*Al Kooper*

ACCEPTING REJECTION

Many times when you get shot down, it's the right decision. I don't take it personally, and I consider where it's coming from. A composer isn't the end all and the final judge of what is right for the picture.

—*Henry Mancini*

Henry Mancini

CAN YOU HANDLE IT?

If you can make it through those times where you're rejected and depressed and you're not in fashion, you're not trendy, you're not hip—then you really know that you're cut out for it.

—*Suzanne Vega*

FAILURE

I would say that the basic characteristic of my life is failure. Since most of the things that I set out to do are theoretically impossible, it's very easy to fail. I've learned to live with it.

—*Frank Zappa*

PREPARE TO FAIL, BUT DON'T FAIL TO PREPARE

If you're not prepared to fail, then you're in the wrong business. The next record could sell two copies, one to my brother and one to my mother, and that might be it. I have to accept that as easily and as comfortably as I accept any kind of success.

—*Jann Arden*

Jann Arden

PLACES

MAKING IT AT HOME

In Belgium, I became the "local son does good." I have that stamp of approval, but it took thirty years. I was accepted in Sweden before I was popular in Belgium. Somehow the Belgians are skeptical. To become famous, you have to sleep with a famous lady, win a bicycle race, or be a great soccer player.

—*Toots Thielemans*

AMERICA DREAMING

I came from white-washed Austria, where we really didn't have many black people on the streets. I was very much a jazz-influenced guy; all my heroes were Americans. Most of them were black. I wanted nothing more than to become a black musician.

—*Peter Wolf*

Peter Wolf

IF YOU'RE GOING TO...

San Francisco acts as a magnet that draws people into a small place. They're thrown together and forced to interact with one another on both positive and negative levels. You get a lot out of a little time in San Francisco.

—*Paul Kantner*

IT'S A FREE COUNTRY

If you've done one thing very successfully and it brings fame, you have a platform—but you can still fall flat on your face. It's a risk. You can get stabbed in the back trying new things, especially in England. Luckily, in America, it's not like that. People don't mind you trying out new things. It's a much better atmosphere.

—Andy Summers

NORTHERN LIGHTS

I used to feel that everything in the northern hemisphere was incredible. There were gods, like the Beatles, the Kinks, and the British bands. I suppose I thought that they were even greater than they really were, because they were "up there." I was striving to reach those standards.

—Tim Finn

Tim Finn

PUBLIC EXPOSURE

I'm not the kind of artist who works well in complete isolation. What makes me happiest as an artist is to see other people making things, and that's very easy to do in New York. It's everywhere.

—Laurie Anderson

WORLD MUSIC

The power of American music and its culture overwhelms those in other countries. I'd like to hear more bands from other countries come up with material drawing from their own cultures and synthesizing it into their music.

—Bill Payne

RECREATION

I listen to Mexican radio because I can pretend I'm on vacation.

—Mark Mothersbaugh

GO FIGURE

THE IRONY AND THE ECSTASY

Our second album, in 1968, was my version of an anti-psychedelic record, which is completely the reverse of what it represented to the people who bought it and liked it. In hindsight, had it not been for that, I'm sure we would have never survived the time. It just shows to go ya that no matter where you go and what you do in this industry, things can get distorted so quickly.

—*Dr. John*

TOGETHERNESS, OR LACK THEREOF

I remember a session with a guitar player and a drummer who played on the same album. I said, "You guys must know each other; you were on the same album." "No, we've been on the same albums many times, but we never met before." I thought, how crazy can it get?

—*George Martin*

TIMING IS EVERYTHING

I received the New York State Small Businessman of the Year Award in 1970, at exactly the time that I was losing control of my old company.

—*Robert Moog*

Robert Moog

NEW RAGE

If I find the person who coined the term New Age, I would like to nail his forehead to the wall.

—*Will Ackerman*

AGAINST THE ODDS

For an industry that makes so many records a week, a year, it's amazing that anything is heard more than a few times.

—*Phil Ramone*

GOOFING ON THE BOSS

When I produced Meatloaf's *Bat Out of Hell*, I did it because it didn't seem like any other producer would do it with any enthusiasm. I approached the whole album as being a spoof on Bruce Springsteen. The songs were so freakin' long, but that was what sold it in the end—long songs with goofy punch lines.

—*Todd Rundgren*

Todd Rungren

I ONLY WRITE ABOUT SURFING

I don't know how to surf. I tried once, and the board shot by my head— almost hit me. Scared me so bad, I never tried again.

—*Brian Wilson*

IT'S GREEK TO ME

I don't like reading manuals. They hurt my feelings.

—*Dweezil Zappa*

MUSIC VS. ART

Nobody who shakes up the music world lasts. The music world doesn't desire to be shaken up. In the art world, they look for the novelty that will create a scandal, but the world of music is not the "world of art." It's a world of business.

—*Frank Zappa*

Dweezil Zappa

FOR YOUR EARS ONLY

Were the Beatles putting subliminal messages on their records? Nonsense, not true.

—*Geoff Emerick*

YA GOTTA CHOOSE

I told my parents that I wanted to be a musician when I grew up. And they told me, I had to pick one or the other.

—*Led Ka'apana*

THE SOUND OF INNOCENCE

I really believe that people often do their best work on demos. There is something warm about demos, something innocent.

—*David Tickle*

Led Ka'apana

SLUR IT

I was never known as a rock singer, when I started, because I enunciated too well. They kept saying, "No, slur it. You can *understand* everything."
—*Fee Waybill*

NOW YOU KNOW

John Lennon and I were in a club one night, and I asked him what was their worst song. He looked at me and said, "'Run for Your Life.' It was a piece of shit."
—*Mark Hudson*

GOING LO-FI

I spend an inordinate amount of money to stay away from any sort of technology. I really like the sounds that you get through cheaper equipment.
—*Tom Petty*

ACCORDION TO AL

I think the accordion will completely take over the music industry before long. Synthesizers and electric guitars are going to be passé, and accordion bands are going to spring up all over. I'm happy to be at the forefront of the movement.
—*"Weird Al" Yankovic*

BLESS THE HARMONICA

The harmonica is one of the few instruments that can create a mood all by itself. When a guy waits for the electric chair in the prison cell, you're not going to hear a violin playing all by itself, or a piano. The harmonica somehow can create a mood. I don't

Toots Thielemans

know how, but I'm happy it does, 'cause it got me a few jobs.
—*Toots Thielemans*

7

HEART AND SOUL

FINDING BALANCE

BE, HEAR, NOW

As long as you are enjoying the exact moment you are in, everything will be just fine. Don't have too many expectations.
—*Jack Johnson*

MUSICAL HEALING

The better I am in tune with myself, the better my music will be.
—*Patrick Monahan*

MUSICAL HEALTH

Music is just peace for me. I heal from it. I thrive on it. I need it really badly.
—*Brian Wilson*

MUSIC'S THE THING

People tell me my music is relaxing, and I have a need for that. I don't try to make relaxing music, but I do love balance and security. Music is the thing that keeps me balanced.
—*Suzanne Ciani*

Brian Wilson

THE BASICS

Music is a deep part of my culture. You have your family, your work, your ceremony, and your music.

—*Taj Mahal*

TAKE IT EASY

The wars of the world don't come from outer space. People create them—people who have a war within themselves. I want to create music that eases the war within.

—*Kitaro*

THE FEEL

In music, ninety percent of it is what feels good and sounds good, and then ten percent is about all the rest of it.

—*Robbie Robertson*

Kitaro

IN THE MOMENT

I spend pretty much every waking hour thinking about music in one way or another. You just can't speed up, you have to hang in there and live your life, and let the events of your life feed what you are as a musician. And try to enjoy it all while it's happening.

—*Pat Metheny*

BALANCING ACT

I make my biggest mistakes trying to balance my libido with my superego.

—*Mark Mothersbaugh*

Mark Mothersbaugh

SURFING IS MY RELEASE

You're on the phone, you're doing promotion, you're working all day long, and then you go out and sit on the ocean for a couple of hours and become normal.

—*Chris Isaak*

BACKUP PLAN

Sailing keeps me sane, because I believe that if it all fell through tomorrow, I could go back to fishin'. I'd miss making records, but it wouldn't be the end of my life.

—*Jimmy Buffett*

THE SPIRIT OF MUSIC

If I weren't an optimist, I wouldn't bother being here making a record. The problems that face us are overwhelming. But I look in the faces of my kids, and I get a sense of hope.

—*Graham Nash*

Graham Nash

HEALTH, HAPPINESS, AND GOOD KARMA

KEEPING ART IN YOUR MUSIC

The only art is when you enhance life. Our band loves the dignity of mankind, wherever it is. That's what this band is about, and we would like to relate that to people. You play music with people you like, and you should have a good time.

—*Carlos Santana*

Carlos Santana

CAN'T FOOL THE AUDIENCE

What'll keep you good is to enjoy what you're doing. You can't fool the audience. If you're not enjoying it, it really won't sound good.

—*Tom Petty*

PAYBACK

I believe that there is a responsibility for any artist who takes from other cultures to help to promote the artists and the music that they are in turn inspired by.

—*Peter Gabriel*

BE VALUABLE

You have to feel within yourself that you have something to offer. If you don't feel that you really have something that you need to say, then you should try another profession.

—*Suzanne Vega*

SPREAD THE WEALTH

I have been fortunate to do many things in this profession, which is something that I cherish very highly. And as much as I love it, I want others with talent to have the opportunities.

—*Stevie Wonder*

THE FUTURE OF MUSIC

If I can influence a kid to get into music in a positive way, that's good for all of us.

—*Cesar Rosas*

Cesar Rosas

PLAY RESPONSIBLY

Good players shouldn't drink. Some have, but it will finally interfere with your playing. People used to offer me a drink when I was working, and I'd say, "I've got enough trouble doing this sober."

—*Artie Shaw*

SPIRITUALITY

KEEPING FOCUS

I've always believed that age is a state of mind. We age ourselves only in the ways that our spirit is aged. The meat may decay, but the spirit never will. As long as we keep some focus on the spirit, we're doin' alright.

—*Dr. John*

MESSAGE FROM A FRIEND

A songwriter friend of mine in Dublin, Mick Christopher, fell down some stairs and died. Friends gathered at his grave and, just as we were playing one of his songs, we looked up to the sky and there was a huge, unmistakable "X" right over our heads, made by the clouds. The song was very hopeful, and encouraging—get up off your arse and be the best person you can be.

—*Gemma Hayes*

Gemma Hayes

THANKS BE

Buddhism has made me automatically feel compelled to acknowledge another human being if someone taps me on the shoulder, or stretches out his hand to shake mine. You must respect people, and I realize that my popularity came about because people bought my records. The least I can do is shake their hand.

—*Herbie Hancock*

MUSICAL ENERGY

My musical style has been translated as "new science." It means more than science, though; it means spirit—a return to the spirit. It really means *shizen*—nature. There is big energy, and we move in it. This is the principle that I try to understand and use in my work. It is science, it is spirit, it is religion—everything. Finally, these concepts become one. Creating music is using this energy to communicate with an audience.

—*Kitaro*

OPENING DOORS

Once you've opened the doors of perception, they stay open. It's not a revolving door where you go outside for a little while, and say, "Hey, I'm one with the universe," and then go back inside and become locked up like you were.

—*Ray Manzarek*

THE FORCE IS WITH YOU

The spirit is a very vibrant force. It's like the sap in a tree. Sometimes we go through weather where it doesn't rain for a long time, but the tree is still there. The sap is making the tree hold on 'til the next rainfall.

—*Carlos Santana*

NATURE

There are feelings that come to you when you are under the influence of nature—the magic of nature. You're in God's hands. I've had the feelings many times, ever since I was little— just being there, smelling the breeze, the outdoors, the greenery. There is nothing like that feeling.

—*Stevie Wonder*

Stevie Wonder

SOMEBODY UP THERE LIKES ME

Sometimes, I feel like I didn't have all the control over the records I produced. I thought there was somebody up there in heaven that was pulling my strings.

—*Brian Wilson*

SEARCHING FOR MEANING

It doesn't disappoint me anymore that I don't really know what's going on, and I don't feel as compelled to figure it out. It dawned on me somewhere along the line that no one has, and everyone has tried.

—*Leo Kottke*

FINDING PURPOSE

I don't go to church, and I'm not religious, but I believe in spirit. I have this connected feeling, and I really believe there is something bigger than me out there. I give myself over and say, "Let me do the work— allow that to come through me as a vessel, as a worker." That's what I've done in my own private way, and by doing that, amazing things have happened.

—*David Tickle*

KNOCKIN' ON HEAVEN'S DOOR

I spent two years with Bob Dylan on tour, at the peak of his experience with Jesus. It was a very powerful time in my life, and I could see it was an extremely powerful time in his. I actually saw him change from being pretty hard to be around to a guy that was incredibly open and wonderful to be around.

—*Jim Keltner*

Jim Keltner

HIGHER POWER TOOLS

I believe in God's guidance. I *don't* think He turns the page of the book for you and points out the circuit. There is nothing miraculous in that sense, but if you are prepared to put in the hard work, you get results.

—*Rupert Neve*

AND IN THE END

BELIEVE

I was told by my pa that it is better to believe than to not believe. If you croak and you find out that everything you heard was true, then you're okay.

—Dr. John

CALLING IT QUITS

I always vowed I would bow out gracefully. It's a good thing to do. Otherwise you're out there with a flannel shirt and Speedos onstage at age sixty—not nice!

—Al Kooper

Al Kooper

ARE WE DONE YET?

You never know in this business if you're retired. I've thought a few times I was finished, but then another gig comes up and I go, "No, I guess I'm not retired yet."

—Duane Eddy

WHAT GOES UP

No one can have hit records all the time. I can't think of anybody that has defied this fact of life. There seems to come a time when it just doesn't work anymore for an artist.

—*David Foster*

HOW IT SOUNDS

In terms of records—when it's done, all that will be remembered is how the record sounds.

—*Nathaniel Kunkel*

KNOWING WHEN TO SAY WHEN

In a band, there are times when you want to leave, when you want to work on your own. But the hold that a band has on you, psychologically, makes it tough to make the break. I found peace within myself to say, "I've taken this about as far as I can, and I want to do something else."

—*Bill Payne*

KEEPIN' ON

I'm still growing, and I hope to grow until the day I die. And then I hope that what I leave behind will grow through someone else and become better than where I was able to take it.

—*Stevie Wonder*

ART AND LOVE

I think all art is a manifestation of love, and art is transcendent, so love is a timeless thing.

—*Sean Lennon*

Sean Lennon

AUTHOR'S ACKNOWLEDGMENTS

The author would first like to thank David Schwartz, who boldly published Mr. Bonzai's original studio memoirs, which led to a long-range career as interviewer and photojournalist. He would especially like to thank all of the subjects in this book, and the publications which have printed his words and photos: *Mix*, *EQ*, *Sound & Recording*, *Electronic Musician*, *Rolling Stone*, *New York Times*, *Los Angeles Times*, *Hollywood Reporter*, *Daily Variety*, *Computer Life*, *Billboard*, *Pro Sound News*, *Keyboard*, *Bass Player*, and *Surfer's Path*.

In addition, the author gives thanks to these individuals who have encouraged his work: Kit Alexander, Jane Ayer, Bryan Bell, Sarah Benzuly, Eva Böhm, Jeff Evans, Jonathan "Gus" Feist, Heidi Robinson Fitzgerald, Marty Porter, John Fry, David Hockney, Greg Hofmann, Blair Jackson, Michael Jensen, Barry Kelly, Dave Kusek, John Lennon, Dave Lockwood, Curt Lyon, Norman MacCaig, Bruce Maddocks, Miki Nakayama, Jim Pace, Rick Plushner, Brad Smith, Geoff Stirling, Kamran V, Carloquinto Talamona, Chögyam Trungpa, Paul Verna, Christopher Walsh, Alan Wedertz, and Frank Wells.

ABOUT THE AUTHOR/ PHOTOGRAPHER

Award-winning photographer, jour-
nalist, and author, Mr. Bonzai is a graduate of the University of California,
B.A. English Literature with minor in
Art & Film. After college, he was a
writer/performer in the improvisational Praxis Theater, and co-founded
"Strangemouth," a radio comedy
group which broadcast live in the U.S.
and Canada. As creative director of

Mr. Bonzai
Photo: Peter Wolf

Canada's top-rated CHOM-FM, he served as announcer, writer, and
producer, and upon his return to the U.S., managed Lyon Recording
Studios, also operating as in-house producer/announcer/engineer.

Since 1980, Mr. Bonzai has written over 1,000 articles for magazines in
the U.S., Europe and Asia, including photographs and over 500 interviews with leading musicians, artists, directors, producers, and media
figures. In 2006, he published *FACES of MUSIC: 25 Years of Lunching
with Legends.*

Visit Mr. Bonzai's Web site at www.mrbonzai.com.

ABOUT THE EDITOR

David Schwartz's fascination with music making began when he was exposed to classical music as a small child, watching his father rehearse his timpani part for his next symphony concert. After earning degrees in engineering and business, David pursued his first love and joined Wally Heider Recording Studios, in San Francisco, where he had a working view of many of his favorite recording artists in their

David Schwartz
Photo: Cathy M. Callanan

creative chambers. This experience triggered his desire to shine the light on the great, but underappreciated, work of studio engineers and producers, leading him to focus on their contributions in the pages of *Mix* magazine, which he co-founded in 1976.

It was during his early days as editor in chief of *Mix* that he had an "extraordinary encounter" with Mr. Bonzai, the circumstances of which made it clear to both of them that they would enjoy a long and creative relationship. This is the third book they have co-developed, after *Studio Life* and *Hal Blaine and the Wrecking Crew*.

WHO'S WHO

Ackerman, Will	Recording artist. Co-founder, Windham Hill Records
Alagia, John	Engineer, producer. Credits: Liz Phair, Dave Matthews
Allen, Steve	Pianist, lyricist, humorist, television personality
Allison, Mose	Jazz pianist, songwriter
Alpert, Herb	Producer, trumpeter, co-founder A&M Records
Anderson, Laurie	Recording artist
Arden, Jann	Singer, songwriter. Canadian Juno Award-winner
Asher, Peter	Producer, artist. Credits: Linda Ronstadt, James Taylor
Ballard, Glen	Producer. Credits: No Doubt, Aerosmith, Van Halen
Becker, Terry	Engineer. Credits: Jackson Browne, Bonnie Raitt, the Band
Becker, Walter	Co-founder, Steely Dan
Benson, Ray	Singer, songwriter, producer. Founder. Asleep at the Wheel
Biller, Tom	Engineer, producer. Credits: Fiona Apple, Jon Brion
Blaine, Hal	Studio drummer on more than forty number 1 songs
Blake, Tchad	Engineer, producer. Credits: Sheryl Crow, Los Lobos
Bohm, Martin	Engineer, studio owner. Credits: Bono, Marianne Faithfull
Botnick, Bruce	Engineer, producer. Credits: the Doors, the Turtles, the Beach Boys
Brion, Jon	Recording artist, producer. Credits: Kanye West, Fiona Apple
Browder, Sally	Engineer. Credits: Plimsouls, Eliades Ochoa, Dwight Yoakum
Browne, Jackson	Singer, songwriter
Buckingham, Lindsey	Singer, songwriter, guitarist. Member of Fleetwood Mac
Buffett, Jimmy	Singer, songwriter
Carranza, Robert	Engineer, producer. Credits: Jack Johnson, Ozomatli
Cathcart, Patti	Singer, songwriter. Member of Tuck and Patti
Cherney, Ed	Engineer, producer. Credits: the Rolling Stones, Bonnie Raitt
Chiccarelli, Joe	Engineer, producer. Credits: the White Stripes, Beck, Elton John
Ciani, Suzanne	Pianist, recording artist
Clearmountain, Bob	Mixing engineer. Credits: Bruce Springsteen, Bryan Adams
Cohen, Leonard	Singer, songwriter, author, poet
Coleman, Lisa	Composer, musician. Member of Prince's band, Wendy & Lisa
Connick Jr., Harry	Singer, recording artist
Copeland, Stewart	Drummer, the Police
Coppola, Carmine	Film composer. Credits: *Apocalypse Now*, *Godfather III*
Coss, Stevie	Composer, producer. Credits: Morton, Missy May
Crenshaw, Marshall	Singer, songwriter
Criss, Peter	Drummer of Kiss
Cropper, Steve	Studio guitarist, songwriter
DeLena, Eddie	Engineer. Credits: Michael Jackson, Mick Jagger, Queen
Dolby, Thomas	Singer, songwriter, recording artist
Douglas, Steve	Studio saxophonist
Dr. John	Singer, songwriter, pianist, recording artist
Duke, George	Composer, keyboardist, producer. Credits: Mothers of Invention

Eddy, Duane	Guitarist, recording artist
Elfman, Danny	Film composer. Credits: *Batman, Men in Black, Dick Tracy*
Emerick, Geoff	Engineer. Credits: the Beatles, America, Badfinger, Supertramp
Fair, Ron	Producer. Credits: Christina Aguilera, Pussycat Dolls
Finn, Neil	Singer, songwriter. Member of Crowded House, Split Enz
Finn, Tim	Singer, songwriter. Member of Crowded House, Split Enz
Flea	Bassist. Member of the Red Hot Chili Peppers
Foster, David	Producer. Credits: Chicago, Celine Dion, Whitney Houston
Froom, Mitchell	Engineer, producer. Credits: Sheryl Crow, Crowded House
Gabriel, Peter	Singer, songwriter, recording artist. Member of Genesis
Grundman, Bernie	Mastering engineer. Credits: Michael Jackson, Steely Dan, Jack Johnson
Hancock, Herbie	Musician, recording artist
Herschberg, Lee	Engineer. Credits: James Taylor, Randy Newman
Herzberg, Tal	Engineer. Credits: Green Day, Pink, David Bowie
Hidalgo, David	Singer, guitarist. Member of Los Lobos
Hite, Silas	Composer. Credits: *Shaggy and Scooby Doo Get a Clue*
Holland, Brian	Songwriter. Credits: the Four Tops, the Supremes, the Temptations
Hormel, Geordie	Composer, engineer, studio owner: The Village
Horn, Paul	Jazz flutist, recording artist
Höskulds, S. "Husky"	Engineer. Credits: Tom Waits, Sheryl Crow, Gipsy Kings
Hudson, Mark	Musician, songwriter, producer. Credits: Ringo, Aerosmith
Isaak, Chris	Singer, songwriter, recording artist
Isham, Mark	Film composer. Credits: *Rules of Engagement, The Cooler*
Jarre, Maurice	Film composer. Credits: *Dr. Zhivago, Lawrence of Arabia*
Johnson, Jack	Singer, songwriter, recording artist
Jones, Booker T.	Keyboardist, producer, recording artist
Jones, Rickie Lee	Singer, songwriter, recording artist
Ka'apana, Led	Singer, songwriter, master of slack key guitar
Kantner, Paul	Songwriter. Member of Jefferson Airplane
Keltner, Jim	Studio drummer. Credits: John Lennon, Bob Dylan
Kershenbaum, David	Producer. Credits: Tracy Chapman, Joan Baez, Joe Jackson
Kiedis, Anthony	Singer, songwriter. Member of Red Hot Chili Peppers
Killen, Kevin	Engineer. Credits: U2, Peter Gabriel, Jewel
King, B.B.	Blues guitarist, recording artist
Kitaro	Synthesist, recording artist, film composer
Kooper, Al	Songwriter, keyboardist, producer. Founder of Blood Sweat and Tears, the Blues Project
Kortchmar, Danny	Guitarist, songwriter, producer. Credits: Don Henley, James Taylor, Carole King
Kottke, Leo	Guitarist, recording artist
Kramer, Eddie	Engineer. Credits: the Beatles, Jimi Hendrix, Led Zeppelin
Kristofferson, Kris	Singer, songwriter, recording artist
Kunkel, Nathaniel	Engineer. Credits: Graham Nash, David Crosby, Sting

Ladanyi, Greg	Engineer, producer. Credits: Jackson Browne, Fleetwood Mac
Lagadec, Roger	Digital audio scientist
Lamm, Robert	Songwriter, singer, keyboardist. Member of Chicago
lang, k.d.	Singer, songwriter, recording artist
Lennon, John	Singer, songwriter, recording artist. Member of the Beatles
Lennon, Sean	Singer, songwriter, recording artist
Lindley, David	Guitarist, recording artist. Credits: Jackson Browne, Ry Cooder, Rod Stewart
Lovett, Lyle	Singer, songwriter, recording artist
Lukather, Steve	Guitarist. Member of Toto
Lynch, David	Film and television director, composer, musician
Lynne, Jeff	Guitarist, producer. Founded Electric Light Orchestra
Mahal, Taj	Singer, songwriter, recording artist
Mancini, Henry	Film composer. Credits: *The Pink Panther*, *Peter Gunn*
Manzarek, Ray	Composer, keyboardist. Member of the Doors
Martin, George	Record Producer. Credits: the Beatles, America
Massenburg, George	Recording engineer, producer, scientist, inventor
McDonald, Michael	Singer, songwriter, recording artist
McKean, Michael	Comedian, composer, musician. Member of Spinal Tap
McRae, Tom	Singer, songwriter, recording artist
Melvoin, Wendy	Composer, musician. Member of Prince's band, Wendy & Lisa
Metheny, Pat	Guitarist, recording artist
Miller, Steve	Singer, songwriter, recording artist
Monahan, Patrick	Singer, songwriter. Member of Train
Moog, Robert	Inventor of Moog Synthesizer
Mothersbaugh, Mark	Film composer. Member of Devo
Nash, Graham	Singer, songwriter. Member of Crosby, Stills, and Nash
Neff, John	Engineer, bass player. Credits: David Lynch films
Nelson, Willie	Singer, songwriter, recording artist
Neve, Rupert	Engineer, inventor, manufacturer
Nichols, Roger	Engineer. Credits: Steely Dan, John Denver
Nilsson, Harry	Singer, songwriter, recording artist
Nitzsche, Jack	Songwriter, arranger, composer. Credits: *Performance*
Offord, Eddy	Engineer, producer. Credits: Yes; Emerson, Lake and Palmer
Padgham, Hugh	Engineer, producer. Credits: the Police, Sting, Phil Collins
Paley, Andy	Songwriter, producer. Credits: Brian Wilson, Sponge Bob
Parks, Van Dyke	Songwriter, composer, recording artist
Parsons, Alan	Engineer, recording artist. Credits: the Beatles, Pink Floyd
Paterno, John	Engineer, producer. Credits: Los Lobos, Sheryl Crow
Paul, Les	Guitarist, artist, inventor of solid body electric guitar
Paul, Stephen	Microphone expert, singer, songwriter, engineer
Payne, Bill	Keyboardist. Member of Little Feat
Perez, Louie	Singer, songwriter, drummer. Member of Los Lobos
Perry, Linda	Songwriter, producer. Credits: Alicia Keyes, Pink

Petty, Tom	Singer, songwriter, recording artist
Porter, Bill	Engineer. Credits: Elvis Presley, Roy Orbison, the Everly Brothers
Ramone, Phil	Producer, engineer. Credits: Billy Joel, Paul Simon, Barbra Streisand
Reitzas, Dave	Engineer. Credits: Madonna, Whitney Houston, Ricky Martin
Robertson, Robbie	Songwriter, guitarist. Member of the Band
Rosas, Cesar	Singer, songwriter, guitarist. Member of Los Lobos
Ross, Michael C.	Engineer. Credits: Mya, Queen Latifa, Herbie Hancock
Rundgren, Todd	Recording artist, songwriter, producer. Credits: Meatloaf
Santana, Carlos	Guitarist, recording artist
Scheiner, Elliot	Recording engineer. Credits: Steely Dan, the Eagles, Queen
Schickele, Peter	Composer, performer, historian. P.D.Q. Bach
Schmitt, Al	Recording engineer. Credits: Frank Sinatra, Jefferson Airplane, Toto
Shaffer, Paul	Keyboardist, bandleader: *Late Show with David Letterman*
Shaw, Artie	Composer, clarinetist, bandleader
Shearer, Harry	Writer, radio personality. Character voices on *The Simpsons*
Shipley, Mike	Engineer. Credits: AC/DC, Cheap Trick, Cars
Sides, Allen	Studio owner, engineer. Credits: Beck, Linda Ronstadt, Eric Clapton
Sklar, Leland	Studio bassist. Credits: James Taylor, Linda Ronstadt, Jackson Browne
Smalls, Derek	aka Harry Shearer. Member of Spinal Tap
Smith, Chad	Drummer of the Red Hot Chili Peppers
St. Hubbins, David	aka Michael McKean. Member of Spinal Tap
Stone, Chris	Co-founder of the Record Plant, founder of World Studio Group
Summers, Andy	Guitarist. Member of the Police
Sutton, Ralph	Engineer. Credits: Stevie Wonder, Michael Jackson, Ice Cube
Swedien, Bruce	Engineer, producer. Credits: Michael Jackson, Count Basie, Jennifer Lopez
Tedesco, Tommy	Studio guitarist
Thielemans, Toots	Jazz harmonica player, recording artist
Thompson, Richard	Singer, songwriter, recording artist
Tickle, David	Engineer, producer. Credits: Prince, U2, Peter Gabriel
Titelman, Russ	Producer. Credits: Eric Clapton, Steve Winwood, Paul Simon
Transeau, Brian "BT"	Composer, re-mixer. Credits: Britney Spears, *NSYNC
Ungar, Leanne	Engineer. Credits: Leonard Cohen, Janis Ian, Willie Nelson
Vai, Steve	Guitarist. Credits: Frank Zappa, David Lee Roth
Vanston, C.J.	Composer, keyboardist, producer. Credits: Joe Cocker, Spinal Tap, Prince
Vega, Suzanne	Singer, songwriter, recording artist
Was, Don	Songwriter, producer, member of Was (Not Was). Credits: the Rolling Stones, Bob Dylan, Bonnie Raitt
Was, David	Songwriter, producer, member of Was (Not Was). Credits: Rickie Lee Jones, Bob Dylan, Holly Cole

Waybill, Fee	Singer. Member of the Tubes
Webb, Jimmy	Songwriter. Credits: *MacArthur Park, Wichita Lineman*
Weinberg, Max	Drummer for the E Street Band, Conan O'Brien bandleader
Weisberg, Tim	Jazz flutist, recording artist
West, James	Composer, guitarist, slack key recording artist. Member of "Weird Al" Yankovic band
Wilson, Brian	Singer, songwriter, recording artist. Co-founder of the Beach Boys
Wolf, Peter	Composer, keyboardist, producer. Credits: Wang Chung, Jefferson Starship, Santana
Wonder, Stevie	Singer, songwriter, recording artist
Woods, Phil	Jazz saxophonist
X, Geza	Composer, producer. Credits: Germs, Black Flag, Redd Kross
Yakus, Shelly	Engineer. Credits: Van Morrison, Tom Petty, Bob Seger
Yankovic, "Weird Al"	Singer, parodist, accordion player, recording artist
Yoakam, Dwight	Singer, songwriter, recording artist
Zappa, Dweezil	Composer, songwriter, guitarist, recording artist
Zappa, Frank	Composer, songwriter, guitarist, recording artist
Zimmer, Hans	Film composer. Credits: *Gladiator, The Lion King, Pirates of the Caribbean*

INDEX

Page numbers in *italics* refer to illustrations and captions.